CW00944787

The Power of
The A1s

When only three months old, No 60127 must have been a superb sight in its blue livery with Pullman coaches on the down 'Queen of Scots', seen crossing the Royal Border Bridge at Berwick in August 1949. No 60127 was the first 'A1' to be painted from new in the blue livery, which was a different shade from that used on *Great Northern*, the garter blue of the 'A4s' and the experimental blue applied to seven Class A3s. *E. R. Wethersett*

The Power of
The A1s

Gavin Morrison

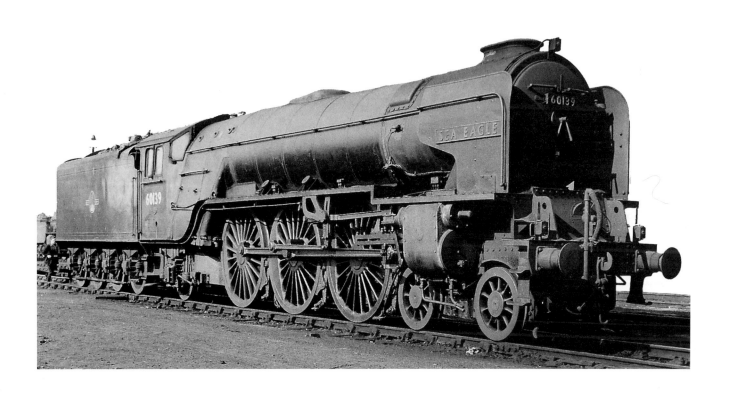

Oxford Publishing Co

Introduction

First published 2000

ISBN 0 86093 552 3

All rights reserved. No part of this book may be reproduced or transmitted in any form or by any means, electronic or mechanical, including photocopying, recording or by any information storage and retrieval system, without permission from the Publisher in writing.

© Ian Allan Publishing Ltd 2000

Published by Oxford Publishing Co

an imprint of Ian Allan Publishing Ltd, Terminal House, Shepperton, Surrey TW17 8AS.
Printed by Ian Allan Printing Ltd, Riverdene Business Park, Hersham, Surrey KT12 4RG.

Code: 0011/B2

Frontispiece:
A fine study of No 60155 *Borderer* heading north across Plawsworth Viaduct with a down express on 1 August 1964. This viaduct used to produce fine pictures in both directions, but today the trees have grown to such an extent that it is hardly visible. *A. R. Thompson*

Bibliography
Locomotives of the LNER, Part 2A, Railway Correspondence & Travel Society
East Coast Pacifics at Work, P. N. Townend, Ian Allan Publishing
The Power of the A1s, A2s and A3s, J. S. Whiteley & G. W. Morrison, Oxford Publishing Co

Acknowledgments
My thanks to the many photographers whose pictures have been used, and to the help given by the members of the A1 Steam Locomotive Trust.

THE 49 Class A1 locomotives attributed to A. H. Peppercorn were actually authorised for construction while Thompson was still in charge at Doncaster. On 25 October 1945, 16 were authorised to be built at Doncaster, and a further 23 in the 1946 building programme at Darlington. The remaining 10 were built during 1949 at Doncaster.

Thompson's choice of Sir Nigel Gresley's original 'A1', *Great Northern*, for rebuilding was considered controversial by many, and some pressure was brought to bear on Thompson (without success) to select another locomotive. However, once the rebuilt locomotive had entered traffic, it had to be admitted that its performance was as good as or even better than that of the other Gresley Pacifics, even if its appearance found little favour. Over the years it gave good service at many sheds, in spite of being a one-off locomotive.

Now, around 35 years since the last 'A1' was withdrawn, it is clear that these were very fine locomotives, capable of extremely hard work, they steamed superbly, clocked up very high mileages between overhauls, and were complete masters of the work allocated to them. In the earlier days their riding qualities gave many crews cause for concern, and much has been written about the reasons and remedies in other publications. Recordings of speeds of 100mph and over are relatively rare by comparison with the Class A4s; the highest I ever recorded was 94mph down to Stoke Bank on the up 'Queen of Scots'.

During their entire career the 'A1s' lived under a cloud created by the publicity afforded to the 'A4s' and the superb high-speed exploits in the prewar years, but as none of the class was ever fitted with a corridor tender they never had the opportunity to grab the limelight on prestigious workings such as the 'Capitals Limited' or 'Elizabethan'. I am certain that the King's Cross-allocated, roller-bearing-fitted 'A1s' Nos 60156 and 60157 would have performed well had they been given the opportunity.

The West Riding of Yorkshire to King's Cross services became the regular duties of the 'A1s' allocated to Copley Hill at Leeds, where some fine work was put in on trains such as the 'West Riding', 'Yorkshire Pullman' and 'Queen of Scots', but it is possible that the performances achieved by the two Gateshead-allocated roller-bearing locomotives Nos 60154 and 60155 were the finest ever by the class. These two locomotives were allocated to the 'Night

Scotsman' services, which they worked consistently for five years, going up one night to King's Cross and returning the next. They would often complete a round trip to Edinburgh during the day, and King's Cross often borrowed them for a return trip to Peterborough during their layover, resulting in daily mileages in excess of 500. These duties never hit the headlines, but must have constituted some of the finest express work ever performed on British Railways.

The class had a very short career, enjoying barely 10 years on top-link workings before diesels took over. The introduction of the Class 55 'Deltics' from 1961 onwards soon relegated them to secondary duties, but some fine performances were achieved in the 1960s, often standing in for failed diesels.

The class was involved in remarkably few accidents, although No 60123 *H. A. Ivatt* became the first to be withdrawn, after an accident near Offord in September 1962. Withdrawals came swiftly during 1964, until all had gone by June 1966. There was little suitable work for them in the last couple of years, and it was common to find over half a dozen at York shed, all well cleaned but not in steam, during 1965.

The 'A1s' seldom ventured far off the main East Coast routes, although some locomotives had short spells at Polmadie (Glasgow) during the early 1950s, and others were

Above:
No 60141 *Abbotsford*, considered to be the best of Copley Hill depot's 'A1s' in the early 1960s, gets into its stride at the head of the up 'White Rose' at Wortley Junction South, Leeds, on 7 June 1962. *Gavin Morrison*

to be seen on the Settle–Carlisle and Glasgow & South Western lines from 1964 onwards, usually on summer relief workings, the locomotives involved being allocated to Neville Hill. The last Doncaster-based members of the class were regularly allocated to three-coach all-stations workings to Leeds in 1965. They were fine locomotives which did not really have the opportunity, due to their short careers, to receive all the praise that was bestowed upon the Gresley Pacifics.

Exciting times are yet to come for the 'A1' class, when its 50th member, No 60163 *Tornado*, takes to the main line in a few years time and, with the benefit of modern technology employed in its construction at Darlington, it may eventually prove to be the finest Pacific to run on the railways of Britain.

G. W. Morrison
October 2000

4470 / 60113 *Great Northern*

Built	Doncaster April 1922; rebuilt Doncaster September 1945
Liveries after rebuilding	Originally Royal blue with red lining
	LNER apple green May 1947
	BR blue January 1950
	BR green August 1952
Allocations when rebuilt	Doncaster September 1945
	King's Cross October 1945
	Gateshead July 1947
	Haymarket September 1947
	King's Cross September 1947
	New England June 1950
	Grantham September 1951
	King's Cross September 1957
	Doncaster October 1957
Withdrawn	November 1962; scrapped Doncaster

Below:
This is an official picture of *Great Northern* painted in the Royal blue livery with red lining, as it emerged from Doncaster Works in September 1945, with the short cab and no smoke deflectors. Very little of the original Gresley Pacific was used — only part of the cab and wheel centres — making it virtually a new locomotive. It had the longest wheelbase of any Pacific built by the LNER to this date, at 38ft 5in. The boiler was standard with the 'A4' diagram 107. *Ian Allan Library*

Bottom:
After only three months, *Great Northern* received smoke deflectors and an altered cab, improving the appearance of the locomotive. This picture was dated 28 September 1946, showing the locomotive in Royal blue livery. The location is Hadley Wood. *H. C. Casserley*

Right:
A fine picture of *Great Northern* taken on 25 June 1946, about to leave King's Cross on a down express, in its impressive blue livery. *C. C. B. Herbert*

Below:
Another picture of *Great Northern* at King's Cross taken nine months later on 18 March 1947, ready to leave with an express at 10.10am. The locomotive has now received No 113, but is looking in poor external condition. It was during September of 1947 that *Great Northern* was sent to Haymarket and tested against single-chimney 'A4' No 31 *Golden Plover*. The 'A1' consumed less coal and water than the 'A4' and performed well, but was prone to slipping when working hard and leaving certain stations. *C. C. B. Herbert*

Below:
The portrait of the first Great Northern Railway Chairman, Michael Denison, adorns the impressive headboard as *Great Northern* appropriately heads the Centenary Special from King's Cross to York on 16 July 1950. Note 'New England' on the buffer-beam, where the locomotive was allocated for 15 months at this time. *E. R. Wethersett*

Above:
Great Northern with another prominent headboard, this time advertising the Northern Rubber Co. The locomotive must have looked impressive in its BR blue livery as it passed Potters Bar on its way north on 8 September 1951. *E. R. Wethersett*

Right:
A close-up of *Great Northern*'s nameplate and crest, taken when the locomotive was freshly ex-works at Doncaster in the mid-1950s.
Gavin Morrison

Below:
With just over a year to go before withdrawal, *Great Northern* pulls out of Leeds Central on the 2.05pm local service to Doncaster on 9 August 1961. The locomotive in original and rebuilt form lasted 40 years, and covered around 2 million miles. Of these, 950,000 were in rebuilt form over 17 years, giving an average of around 65,000 per annum, which, as P. N. Townend mischievously points out in his book *East Coast Pacifics at Work*, was nearly 10,000 higher than that achieved by Great Western 'Stars' and 'Castles' in a typical year. *Gavin Morrison*

60114 *W. P. Allen*

Built	Doncaster August 1948 (Works No 2031)
Named	28 October 1948
Liveries	Originally LNER apple green with 'British Railways' on tender
	BR blue January 1951
	BR green March 1952
Allocations	King's Cross when new
	Copley Hill June 1950
	Grantham February 1953
	Doncaster September 1957
Withdrawn	26 December 1964; sold for scrap to Hughes-Bolckow, Blyth, Febrauary 1965

Above:
An official photograph of No 60114. It emerged from Doncaster Works on 6 August 1948, painted in LNER green livery, but with 'British Railways' on the tender. Comparative trials were carried out in 1949 between No 60114 and Class A2 No 60539 *Bronzino*, with approximately 500-ton loads at first, rising to 600 tons; the conclusion was that, overall, there was very little to choose between the two locomotives. *Ian Allan Library*

Below:
This very fine picture of No 60114 passing New Southgate on a down express is undated, but as the locomotive is still un-named it must have been before 28 October 1948, and must therefore have been virtually brand-new. There is also no indication of its allocation on the buffer-beam, although it was in fact based at King's Cross. *E. R. Wethersett*

Above:

The locomotive has now been named *W. P. Allen*. It was originally intended that the class would not carry names, but an exception was made to honour W. P. Allen, who was the Trade Union member of the Railway executive, the ceremony being carried out by Sir Eustace Missenden, Chairman of the Railway Executive, at King's Cross station on 28 October 1948. No 60114 thus became the only Peppercorn 'A1' to carry a name while still in LNER apple green (although, by the time of this photograph, it had received the short-lived blue livery). Eighteen months later the decision was reversed and the remainder of the class were given names, commencing with No 60133 in April 1950. *Ian Allan Library*

Centre:

The 'A1s' never wandered very far off their regular routes, except in the last few years when they were seen on the Settle–Carlisle, Glasgow & South Western and other lines. On 28 September 1963, *W. P. Allen* made what was possibly the only working of a Class A1 over the Calder Valley main line, on a Blackpool Illuminations special. It is shown in this picture entering Sowerby Bridge station, where it stopped for water. A local landmark, Wainhouse Tower, can be seen above the boiler. *Gavin Morrison*

Below:

This picture of *W. P. Allen*, at Holbeck shed on 4 December 1964, must have been taken only days before the locomotive was withdrawn. Along with other Doncaster-based 'A1s' at this time, it worked stopping trains to Leeds, and was serviced at Holbeck. *Gavin Morrison*

60115 *Meg Merrilies*

Built	Doncaster September 1948 (Works No 2032)
Named	June 1950
Liveries	Originally LNER apple green with 'British Railways' on tender
	BR blue June 1950
	BR green September 1952
Allocations	Gateshead when new
	Copley Hill November 1960
Withdrawn	12 November 1962; scrapped Doncaster 25 May 1963

Below:
Meg Merrilies appears to have been one of the camera-shy members of the class, as this is the earliest picture, which was readily available and was taken on 21 July 1958. The locomotive is seen approaching York on a King's Cross–Glasgow Queen Street train, probably the 'Junior Scotsman'. The class initially gained a reputation for rough riding, and *Meg Merrilies*, along with No 60136, was selected for special tests involving measuring expansion of the frames between the inside and outside cylinders. It was found that expansion of the valve spindle was greater than had been allowed for, and consequently adjustments were made to the whole class to reflect this. *D. C. Ovenden*

During its two-year spell at Copley Hill shed in Leeds, *Meg Merrilies* is shown accelerating the 5.20pm Leeds Central to King's Cross over the London North Western line and yard at Wortley Junction South, Leeds, on 2 June 1961. This was not the best vantage point at Wortley Junction South, but the photographer had been unable to leave the office early enough to get to the trackside by the gantry! *Gavin Morrison*

Kidds
OFFICE EQUIPMENT
117 THE HEADROW LEEDS 1
Tel. 28466

Above:
Meg Merrilies in unfamiliar surroundings at the former
Lancashire & Yorkshire shed at Wakefield (56A) on 7 April
1961. The reason for its visit is unknown, but it was not in
steam. *Gavin Morrison*

Below:
Meg Merrilies at its home shed of Copley Hill on 7 March
1962. *Gavin Morrison*

60116 *Hal o' the Wynd*

Built	Doncaster October 1948 (Works No 2033)
Named	May 1951
Liveries	Originally LNER apple green with 'British Railways' on tender
	BR blue March 1950
	BR green August 1952
Allocations	Heaton when new
	Tweedmouth September 1962
	Gateshead October 1964
Withdrawn	14 June 1965; sold for scrap to Hughes-Bolckow, Blyth, July 1965

Above:
An early picture of No 60116, taken prior to its repaint into blue livery in March 1950.
Ian Allan Library

Right:
Another early view of No 60116, still in apple green, probably at the south end of the East Coast main line on the down 'Tees-Tyne Pullman'.
Ian Allan Library

Below:
A fine picture of No 60116 *Hal o' the Wynd* approaching Penshaw North with a down parcels train which has been diverted via Leamside and Washington due to engineering works on the main line, taken in 1960. *I. S. Carr*

Above:
Hal o' the Wynd, looking shabby in Doncaster Works yard, awaits its turn in the main repair shop on 29 April 1962. *Gavin Morrison*

Below:
Leaving Motherwell on 21 June 1963, *Hal o' the Wynd* heads the 9.50 Euston–Perth, which it had presumably taken over at Carlisle, standing in for the more usual Stanier Pacific. It bears a 52D (Tweedmouth) shedplate, having been transferred there in September 1962 after nearly 14 years at Heaton. *M. Bryce*

60117 *Bois Roussel*

Built	Doncaster October 1948 (Works No 2034)
Named	July 1950
Liveries	Originally LNER apple green with 'British Railways' on tender
	BR blue July 1950
	BR green November 1951
Allocations	Grantham when new
	Copley Hill June 1950
	Grantham May 1952
	Copley Hill February 1953
	Ardsley September 1964
	Gateshead December 1964
	Ardsley January 1965
Withdrawn	21 June 1965; sold for scrap to Clayton & Dawe, Dunstan, August 1965

Above:
No 60117 *Bois Roussel* spent the majority of its working days allocated to Copley Hill, so it is not surprising that the selection of pictures were all taken between Leeds and King's Cross. This fine study of *Bois Roussel* leaving Peterborough on a down excursion on 3 April 1953 has many interesting features besides the locomotive. To the left can be seen Peterborough Cathedral, whilst on the right are the lines past the old Spittal Bridge shed, and in the distance the chimneys of Felton brickworks. The picture also illustrates very well the need for the severe speed restriction imposed at the north end of the station.
P. H. Wells

Right:
A truly classic photograph of the up 'Queen of Scots' passing Wortley Junction South, Leeds, headed by a very clean *Bois Roussel* on 15 April 1954. The crew had obviously been well briefed as to what was required as far as exhaust was concerned, and had done an excellent job. Both driver and fireman are having a quick look out of the cab to check the results of their efforts. Below can be seen the former London & North Western marshalling yards; today an industrial estate occupies this site. It is very rare to have an exact date for one of Eric Treacy's pictures. *Eric Treacy*

Above:

Above:
On 5 April 1959 bridge repairs were taking place at Wortley Junction South, so diversions of Leeds Central–King's Cross expresses were taking place on several Sundays via Bradford and the Lancashire & Yorkshire line via Cleckheaton and Horbury to Wakefield. This picture shows *Bois Roussel* off its normal route as it rounds the sharp curve (part of the triangle just to the west of Low Moor station) onto the Cleckheaton line. It is heading the up 'Harrogate Sunday Pullman', which had arrived at Low Moor via the Bradford avoiding line behind a 'B1' and a Hughes 'Crab', as Pacifics were barred from this route and had to

get to Low Moor by reversing at Bradford Exchange. *Gavin Morrison*

Above:
Another picture of *Bois Roussel* working the diverted 10.45pm King's Cross–Leeds express during the bridge repairs at Wortley Junction South. In this view it is leaving the Lancashire & Yorkshire main line at Thornhill, heading towards Cleckheaton and Low Moor. In the background can be seen Thornhill station, which was to close on 31 December 1961. Today this location has only two lines. *Ian Allan Library*

Left:
During what was probably *Bois Roussel*'s last visit to Doncaster Works, which was as late as 19 May 1963, it is shown in the yard attached to an 'A3' tender. It did not leave the works in this condition. Behind can be seen the front of 'A4' No 60022 *Mallard*, withdrawn the previous month. *Gavin Morrison*

Left:
A fine night picture of *Bois Roussel* at the head of the 6.03pm Leeds Central–King's Cross on 5 January 1965. This was quite possibly the locomotive's last trip, as it was transferred to Ardsley on 3 January and put into store later that month. *J. M. Rayner*

60118 *Archibald Sturrock*

Built	Doncaster November 1948 (Works No 2035)
Named	July 1950
Liveries	Originally LNER apple green with 'British Railways' on tender BR blue May 1950 BR green January 1952
Allocations	Copley Hill when new Ardsley November 1962 Neville Hill July 1963
Withdrawn	4 October 1965; sold for scrap to T. W. Ward, Killamarsh, November 1965

Below:
No 60118 was another class member that was seldom seen north of Leeds, except during the last two years of its career. Always based in the West Riding of Yorkshire, it spent virtually all its time on Leeds–King's Cross expresses. This is an early picture of the locomotive working the 'Yorkshire Pullman', but unfortunately no further details are available. *R. F. Dearden / Ian Allan Library*

Bottom:
Another early picture of No 60118, this time at the head of a local Leeds Central to Doncaster stopping train, passing its home shed of Copley Hill, Leeds. Note the shed name on the buffer-beam as well as the 37B shedplate. The picture is undated, but must have been taken between May and July 1950 as the locomotive ran for only two months unnamed in blue livery. It is possible it was on a running-in turn following its release from Doncaster Works on 10 May 1950. *Eric Treacy*

Right:
Another picture of *Archibald Sturrock* very much on its own territory, this time leaving a dismal Leeds Central station with an evening local train for Doncaster in September 1961. The author was informed by several Copley Hill crews that around this period No 60118 was a particularly rough-riding locomotive compared to the other members allocated to the shed. *J. M. Rayner*

Below
A view of *Archibald Sturrock* away from its usual routes sees it climbing the 1 in 50 gradient out of Bradford Exchange to Bowling Junction, during the period when, on Sundays, Leeds/Bradford-King's Cross trains were diverted via the ex-Lancashire & Yorkshire lines through Cleckheaton and Horbury. Comprising only five coaches, the train from Bradford would join with the Leeds portion at Low Moor, the Pacific working out of Bradford because they were banned from the Bradford avoiding lines between Laisterdyke and Bowling Junction. The photograph was taken on 8 October 1961. *Gavin Morrison*

Right:
Archibald Sturrock in the yard at its home shed of Copley Hill, Leeds, on 25 April 1962. *Gavin Morrison*

Centre right:
It was only during the last two years of its working career, when allocated to Neville Hill shed, that *Archibald Sturrock* was to be seen regularly north of Leeds. Most of its workings at that time tended to be summer extras, and on 4 July 1964 it was photographed crossing Ais Gill viaduct on the Settle & Carlisle at the head of the Summer Saturdays-only CTAC special, which it would have worked through from Scotland. At this time this train was often hauled in both directions by 'A1s' from Neville Hill.
Gavin Morrison

Bottom right:
At the end of the Glasgow Fair holiday, on 1 August 1964, *Archibald Sturrock* descends Beattock Bank at the head of empty stock working 3X05. It had probably worked into Scotland on the CTAC working mentioned in the picture shown above. Its last works visit would be in September 1964 to Darlington, where it received light repairs including attention to a fractured cylinder.
*Paul Riley /
Ian Allan Library*

60119 *Patrick Stirling*

Built	Doncaster November 1948 (Works No 2036)
Named	July 1950
Liveries	Originally LNER apple green with 'British Railways' on tender
	BR blue June 1950
	BR green February 1952
Allocations	Copley Hill when new
	Grantham December 1955
	King's Cross September 1957
	Doncaster August 1958
Withdrawn	31 May 1964; sold for scrap to Cox & Danks, Wadsley Bridge, August 1964

Above:
A fine picture of No 60119 *Patrick Stirling* taken in the mid-1950s during the locomotive's period of allocation to Grantham — note the shed code (35B) on the smokebox. The location is possibly Little Ponton, south of Grantham. *Ian Allan Library*

In immaculate external condition, *Patrick Stirling* heads the up 'Yorkshire Pullman' near Woolmer Green on 16 May 1952, a few months after receiving BR green livery. *E. R. Wethersett / Ian Allan Library*

Above:

Another fine picture of *Patrick Stirling*, ready to leave Leeds Central on the up 'Yorkshire Pullman', before December 1955 whilst allocated to Leeds Copley Hill depot, as indicated by the 37B shedplate. Note the articulated suburban coaches to the left of the picture. Leeds Central station closed on 1 May 1967. *Eric Treacy*

Below:

With only seven months to go before withdrawal, *Patrick Stirling* is looking rather run-down as it waits for its next duty in the yard of York shed along with a Class V2 on 20 October 1963. *Gavin Morrison*

Below:
An early picture of No 60120, at the head of the down 'Tees-Tyne Pullman' near Potters Bar on 14 July 1949 when the locomotive was allocated to King's Cross.
E. R. Wethersett / Ian Allan Library

60120 *Kittiwake*

Built	Doncaster December 1948 (Works No 2037)
Named	May 1950
Liveries	Originally LNER apple green with 'British Railways' on tender
	BR blue March 1950
	BR green October 1951
Allocations	King's Cross when new
	Copley Hill June 1950
	York September 1963
Withdrawn	20 January 1964; cut up at Darlington Works January 1964

Left:
No 60120 at the head of the 3.30pm King's Cross–Newcastle, heading north near Potters Bar on 7 May 1949. This was the second 'A1' to go to King's Cross when new, but it will always be associated with Copley Hill shed at Leeds, where it spent most of its career.
E. R. Wethersett / Ian Allan Library

Right:
Taken between March and May 1950, of No 60120 is un-named and in BR blue livery. It is at the head of the 'Northumbrian', passing through the London suburbs.
Ian Allan Library

Below:
By now named *Kittiwake*, No 60120 makes a fine sight at the head of the 11.20 Leeds Central–King's Cross express as it passes its home shed of Copley Hill on a mixed set of coaches. A local shunter seems unimpressed by the spectacle. The picture is undated but was probably taken c1953.
Eric Treacy

Right:
Having worked the 'Queen of Scots' from King's Cross to Leeds Central, *Kittiwake* reverses into Copley Hill shed past Wortley South signalbox after turning on the triangle on 9 July 1960. The lines at the bottom of the picture formed the direct route to Bradford Exchange, avoiding Leeds Central.
Gavin Morrison

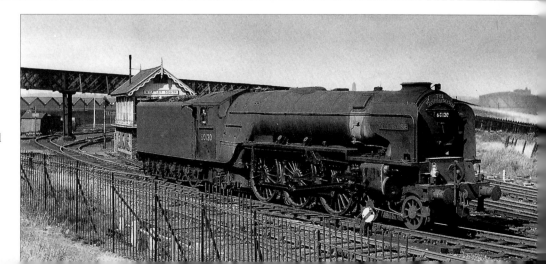

60121 *Silurian*

Built	Doncaster December 1948 (Works No 2038)
Named	May 1950
Liveries	Originally LNER apple green with 'British Railways' on tender
	BR blue May 1950
	BR green December 1951
Allocations	York when new
Withdrawn	4 October 1965; sold for scrap to T. W. Ward, Killamarsh, November 1965

Below:
An early picture of *Silurian*, just two months after being named, and running in BR blue livery. It is at the head of the down 'Yorkshire Pullman', running without a headboard, and is passing New Southgate on 25 July 1950. In keeping with East Coast main line tradition, the locomotive was named after the racehorse which won the Doncaster Cup in 1923.
E. R. Wethersett / Ian Allan Library

Bottom:
Action pictures of *Silurian* are conspicuous by their absence from the author's collection. The first of two portraits taken in 1963 shows the locomotive in the yard at York shed on 20 September. *Gavin Morrison*

Top:
Silurian on 12 October 1963 in the yard of Holbeck shed, Leeds. *Gavin Morrison*

Above:
Silurian received works attention as late as 5 May 1963, when it was photographed outside the paint shop at Doncaster, attached to a Class V2 tender. It is therefore not surprising that this locomotive lasted until October 1965, when no fewer than 10 of the class were withdrawn, leaving just two on the books. *Silurian* was mainly seen south of Newcastle, but in its last two years of service it was observed north of the border. During this period records exist of it on parcels and freight, as well as the more usual passenger workings. *Gavin Morrison*

60122 *Curlew*

Built	Doncaster December 1948 (Works No 2039)
Named	July 1950
Liveries	Originally LNER apple green with 'British Railways' on tender
	BR blue May 1950
	BR green October 1952
Allocations	King's Cross when new
	Grantham September 1951
	Copley Hill October 1953
	Grantham August 1955
	King's Cross September 1957
	Doncaster April 1959
Withdrawn	17 December 1962; cut up Doncaster Works

Below:
A picture taken prior to July 1950 as No 60122 is still un-named, but after May 1950 as it is running in BR blue livery. The locomotive is working hard out of York past the racecourse station with an up express. Note the fine signal gantry and the interesting first coach. *Eric Treacy*

Bottom:
No 60122 was named *Curlew* in July 1950. Believed to be at 'Top Shed', King's Cross, the locomotive was photographed prior to September 1951 when it was transferred to Grantham; this is based on the supposition that Top Shed would not have been cleaning another shed's locomotive. *Eric Treacy*

Above:
Now allocated to Leeds Copley Hill shed, *Curlew* is seen near Wrenthorpe, just to the north of Wakefield Westgate, on a down King's Cross–Leeds express in the mid-1950s. The lines to the right are to Dewsbury and Bradford via Alverthorpe and Ossett. *K. Field*

Right:
Curlew passes through York on 30 August 1958 with the up 'Flying Scotsman', although for some reason the headboard is reversed. The other, rather dirty locomotives are Class A3 No 60080 *Dick Turpin*, of Heaton shed, and LMS 'Jubilee' No 45651 *Shovell*, which was a Bristol Barrow Road locomotive and was probably waiting to take over a Newcastle–Bristol express. *F. Wilde*

Below:
Curlew at its home shed of Doncaster on 29 April 1962. *Gavin Morrison*

60123 *H. A. Ivatt*

Built	Doncaster February 1949 (Works No 2040)
Named	July 1950
Liveries	Originally LNER apple green with 'British Railways' on tender
	BR blue December 1949
	BR green December 1952
Allocations	Doncaster when new
	Grantham March 1950
	Copley Hill June 1950
	Ardsley September 1951
	Copley Hill September 1957
	Ardsley April 1962
Withdrawn	1 October 1962 after accident; cut up
	Doncaster Works 1 October 1962

Above:
This official British Railways photograph, dated 13 July 1950, was no doubt taken at No 60123's official naming ceremony at Doncaster Works; at this time the locomotive was in blue livery and allocated to Copley Hill shed Leeds. *British Railways / Ian Allan Library*

Left:
H. A. Ivatt approaches Retford at the head of a Leeds Central–King's Cross express, the picture being taken from the footbridge. *J. Davenport*

Below:
H. A. Ivatt at the head of the up 'Queen of Scots', passing Beeston Junction on the 1 in 100 climb from Wortley South Junction to Ardsley. In the background can be seen the lines heading off towards Hunslet, avoiding the centre of Leeds, and joining up with the former North Eastern Railway Leeds–York line at Neville Hill. *Eric Treacy*

Right:
On 8 May 1960, *H. A. Ivatt* simmers at the buffer stops at the rather depressing Leeds Central after working the down 'Harrogate Sunday Pullman' from King's Cross. Three coaches would remain in Leeds, whilst the rest of the train headed for Harrogate. The station opened on 18 September 1848 and closed on 1 May 1967. *Gavin Morrison*

Below:
Another view of *H. A. Ivatt* on one of its regular duties, the up 'Queen of Scots', at Wortley South Junction, Leeds, on 9 July 1960. It is just about to cross one of the ex London & North Western routes out of Leeds. Copley Hill shed is just visible, at the other side of the footbridge, as is the town hall clock, in the background on the right.
Gavin Morrison

Right:
H. A. Ivatt became the first member of the class to be withdrawn. It came to a premature end when heading the 8.20pm King's Cross–Leeds at Offord on 7 September 1962. The result of the accident can be seen in this picture taken in the Works yard at Doncaster on 29 September; the locomotive was officially withdrawn on 1 October.
Gavin Morrison

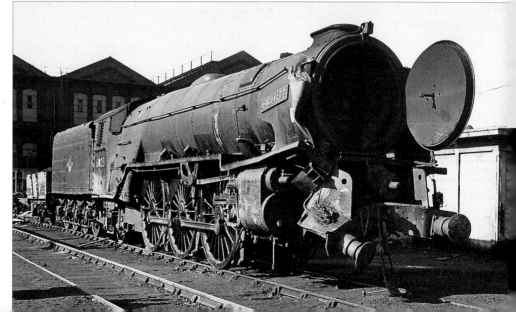

60124 *Kenilworth*

Built	Doncaster March 1949 (Works No 2041)
Named	August 1950
Liveries	Originally LNER apple green with 'British Railways' on tender
	BR blue August 1950
	BR green December 1951
Allocations	Gateshead when new
	Heaton September 1960
	York September 1961
	Darlington November 1964
Withdrawn	27 March 1966; sold for scrap to A. Draper, Hull, May 1966

Below:
With at least 13 coaches behind the tender, No 60124 *Kenilworth* looks in complete control of the up 'Northumbrian' as it leaves Stoke Tunnel on 31 July 1951, at which time it was still in BR blue livery. *E. R. Wethersett*

Left:
Unfortunately this fine picture of *Kenilworth* at the head of the up 'Flying Scotsman' is undated, but was probably taken in the early 1950s. The photographer would likely have had to cover the camera lens to avoid the spray from the water-scoop. *E. R. Wethersett*

Left:
This fine shed shot of *Kenilworth* appears to have been taken at Grantham, probably in the period when most trains to Newcastle and beyond changed locomotives here. Alongside is ex-LNER 'O2' No 63923. *Ian Allan Library*

Below:
On 14 June 1958 *Kenilworth* was in charge of the down 'Heart of Midlothian', which it would have taken over at Grantham. The train is shown at a favourite location for many photographers, alongside the shed yard at York, with the famous Minster in the background. *Gavin Morrison*

Right:
Kenilworth was based at York between September 1961 and November 1964; complete with '50A' shedplate, it is seen on shed in company with 'Britannia' No 70012, which had probably brought an express from Colchester. *Kenilworth*'s last duties were as standby locomotive at Darlington, and it is recorded as having double-headed with 'Deltic' No D9017 on Christmas Eve 1965 from Newcastle to Peterborough. It was the penultimate member of the class, being outlived by No 60145 *Saint Mungo* by three months when the latter was reinstated.
Ian Allan Library

60125 *Scottish Union*

Built	Doncaster April 1949 (Works No 2043)
Named	January 1951
Liveries	Originally LNER apple green with 'British Railways' on tender
	BR blue January 1951
	BR green October 1952
Allocations	Doncaster when new
	Copley Hill June 1950
	Grantham February 1953
	Copley Hill June 1953
	Grantham May 1954
	King's Cross June 1957
	Doncaster January 1958
Withdrawn	4 July 1964; sold for scrap to Cox & Danks, Wadsley Bridge, August 1964

Above:
During its time at Grantham in the mid-1950s, No 60125 *Scottish Union* is seen on Werrington Troughs, at the head of the up 'Talisman'. The lightweight train of eight coaches would have been easy work for the locomotive. *P. Ransome-Wallis*

Right:
Scottish Union off its normal stamping ground as it leaves Low Moor on the ex-Lancashire & Yorkshire line through Cleckheaton to Thornhill, on 12 April 1959. The train is the 1.12pm Leeds to King's Cross, the diversions being due to the closure of the main line around Wortley South Junction, Leeds. Just to the right of the telegraph pole in the centre of the picture can be seen the coaling tower of the ex-Lancashire & Yorkshire shed, by 1959 coded 56F. *K. Field*

Left:
6 June 1962 saw *Scottish Union* at Beeston Junction, Leeds, heading the 10.10am semi-fast to Doncaster and the Eastern Counties. Even as early as 1962 the Doncaster 'A1s' could be seen on these secondary duties. The line to the right avoided the centre of Leeds, rejoining the main line at Neville Hill. The section to Hunslet closed on 30 June 1967. *Gavin Morrison*

Right:
Scottish Union speeds past Sandy at the head of the up 'West Riding' on 7 August 1961 (Bank Holiday). This would normally have been a Copley Hill working, but No 60125 was based at Doncaster by this date. The driver would have been taking advantage of the 1 in 786 downhill stretch of line of just over 1 mile before the virtually continuous uphill section to Stevenage, 15 miles to the south. *M. Mensing*

Centre right:
Scottish Union gets into its stride after stopping at Peterborough on a King's Cross–York express. The picture shows the track layout and yards just north of Peterborough station; in the distance, on the left of the picture, can be seen the coaling towers of New England shed (35A). *P. H. Wells*

Below:
Well coaled up, but with no work allocated as it was not in steam, *Scottish Union* rests on its home shed of Doncaster on 7 April 1963. In spite of its name, the locomotive generally worked on the southern section of the East Coast main line, and visits north of the border would have been infrequent. *Gavin Morrison*

Below:
A fine picture of *Sir Vincent Raven* facing north in the shed yard at York, together with Class V2 No 60981. This picture dates from the early 1950s, as the tender still has the original 'lion and wheel' emblem. *Ian Allan Library*

60126 *Sir Vincent Raven*

Built	Doncaster April 1949 (Works No 2042)
Named	August 1950
Liveries	Originally LNER apple green with 'British Railways' on tender
	BR blue July 1950
	BR green October 1951
Allocations	Heaton when new
	York September 1961
Withdrawn	18 January 1965; sold for scrap to A. Draper, Hull, March 1965

Left:
Now with the later BR emblem, *Sir Vincent Raven* stands on an unidentified shed. *Ian Allan Library*

Right:
Allocated to Heaton for most of its working career, *Sir Vincent Raven* was often seen in Leeds working Liverpool–Newcastle expresses. In a very dirty condition, it receives assistance from Neville Hill-based Standard '4MT' 2-6-4T No 80118 with an evening Liverpool–Newcastle train on 9 July 1960. The train is rounding the curve at Whitehall Junction before taking the Harrogate line and tackling the steep climb to the summit in the 2-mile 741yd Bramhope Tunnel.
Gavin Morrison

Centre right:
Leaking badly, *Sir Vincent Raven* approaches Great Porton on the 1 in 200 climb from Grantham to Stoke Tunnel, at the head of a heavy summer-Saturday express to King's Cross. The station closed to passengers on 15 September 1958, although the freight continued until 29 April 1963. The picture was taken on 7 July 1962.
Gavin Morrison

Left:
Well cleaned and coaled up, but minus the leading tender wheel, *Sir Vincent Raven* stands in the shed yard at York on 12 October 1963. There would have been no urgency to complete the repair as, by this time, York had little work for its 'A1s'.
Gavin Morrison

60127 *Wilson Worsdell*

Built	Doncaster May 1949 (Works No 2044)
Named	September 1950
Liveries	Originally BR blue
	BR green March 1952
Allocations	Heaton when new
	Tweedmouth September 1962
	Gateshead October 1964
Withdrawn	14 July 1965; sold for scrap to Hughes-Bolckow, Blyth, July 1965

Below:
An early view of No 60127, before its naming as *Wilson Worsdell* in September 1950. *Ian Allan Library*

Bottom:
A fine picture of *Wilson Worsdell* passing Essendine on its way to Stoke Summit with a King's Cross–Edinburgh express on 27 February 1954. Essendine station closed to passengers on 15 July 1959, although freight facilities remained until 7 March 1955. *P. H. Wells*

Above:
Few photographs depict 'A1s' double-heading. This picture shows a Birmingham New Street–Newcastle express passing Relly Mill Junction, south of Durham, on 23 June 1956. *Wilson Worsdell* is piloted by 'A2' No 60539 *Bronzino*, both locomotives being allocated to Heaton shed at the time. *I. King*

Below:
Pictures of *Wilson Worsdell* in its later years seem fairly scarce. This undated picture shows the locomotive still with BR's early 'lion and wheel' emblem on the tender. Although Pacifics visited Harrogate virtually every day in the 1950s and early 1960s, photographs are rare. Here No 60127 is about to leave with an express for the North, whilst 'B1' No 61257 waits with a train (probably for York) in the bay platform. *Ian Allan Library*

Below:
A fine early picture of No 60128, taken when the locomotive was only two months old, preparing to leave King's Cross with the 3.45pm 'West Riding' express to Leeds and Bradford on 4 July 1949. The 'A1' was in blue livery, with the coaches in red and cream; note the two front coaches are from a former streamlined train. In the background is 'B1' No 61099. *C. C. B. Herbert*

60128 *Bongrace*

Built	Doncaster May 1949 (Works No 2045)
Named	November 1950
Liveries	Originally BR blue
	BR green February 1952
Allocations	Copley Hill when new
	King's Cross June 1950
	Grantham September 1951
	King's Cross September 1957
	Doncaster April 1959
Withdrawn	10 January 1965; sold for scrap to
	A. Draper, Hull, February 1965

No 60128, now named *Bongrace*, negotiates the complicated trackwork as it arrives at King's Cross with an up express from Leeds on 28 August 1951. *B. K. B. Green*

Right:
Bongrace makes a fine sight as it
accelerates north out of York on the down
'Flying Scotsman'. The shed yard is to the
right of the picture. No date is given, but
the picture was taken after September 1951,
when the locomotive was transferred to
Grantham. *Eric Treacy*

Below:
Bongrace leaves King's Cross with a down
express. *Ian Allan Library*

Left:
Bongrace awaits its
next duty on its
home shed of
Doncaster on
3 March 1963. Note
the oil-cans above
the buffer-beam.
Gavin Morrison

60129 *Guy Mannering*

Built	Doncaster June 1949 (Works No 2046)
Named	November 1950
Liveries	Originally BR blue
	BR green February 1952
Allocations	York when new
	Gateshead September 1949
	Heaton September 1960
	Tweedmouth September 1962
	Gateshead December 1964
	York July 1965
Withdrawn	11 October 1965; sold for scrap to
	R. A. King, Norwich, November 1965

Below:
A superb picture of No 60129 *Guy Mannering* leaving Edinburgh Waverley with the up 'North Briton'. The locomotive appears to have been specially cleaned, possibly for Royal Train duties. No 60129 was the last of the initial batch of 16 locomotives built at Doncaster. *Eric Treacy*

Bottom:
Guy Mannering heads the up 'Flying Scotsman' past the marshalling yards at Dringhouses, just south of York. *Eric Treacy*

Above:
Another picture of *Guy Mannering* at York, this time leaving the north end of the station, with the background dominated by the station hotel.
Eric Treacy

Right:
Although allocated to North Eastern sheds throughout its career, *Guy Mannering* is shown here on the southern section of the East Coast main line at Little Ponton. This undated picture was probably taken in the late 1950s. *J. Davenport*

Bottom right:
With only a couple of months' service remaining, No 60129 looks in a rather run-down condition without its name or works plates as it simmers in the shed yard at York together with WD 2-8-0 No 90517, also allocated to York, on 9 August 1965. On the extreme left is a line of English Electric Type 4 (later Class 40) diesels. No 60129 began and ended its days at York shed, although it is best remembered for its 11 years at Gateshead. *Gavin Morrison*

60130 *Kestrel*

Built	Darlington September 1948 (Works No 2049)
Named	July 1950
Liveries	Originally LNER apple green with 'British Railways' on tender
	BR blue July 1950
	BR green January 1952
Allocations	Doncaster when new
	King's Cross October 1948
	Grantham September 1951
	Ardsley February 1953
	Copley Hill September 1957
	Ardsley September 1964
Withdrawn	4 October 1965; sold for scrap to J. Cashmore, Great Bridge, December 1965

Above:
No 60130 was the first 'A1' to be built at Darlington Works, being completed one month after No 60114 emerged from Doncaster. The visible distinction between the two builds was that the Doncaster locomotives had tenders and cabs with snap-head rivets, whilst the Darlington locomotives had countersunk rivets. This picture shows *Kestrel* ready to leave Grantham at the head of the up 'Northumbrian' during its 17-month allocation to Grantham between September 1951 and February 1953. *Ian Allan Library*

Right:
A highly atmospheric photograph shows *Kestrel* ready to leave King's Cross at the head of the 10.25am to Leeds on a dismal 4 December 1960. *P. H. Wells*

Below:
Kestrel spent 12 of its 17 years allocated to the West Riding sheds of Copley Hill and Ardsley. It is shown at Copley Hill on 19 August 1961, together with King's Cross 'A4' No 60032 *Gannet*.
Gavin Morrison

Bottom left:
Photographed just south of Beeston Junction, *Kestrel* has an easy task at the head of the 4.50pm Leeds Central–Doncaster local. The old trackbed of the former Great Northern line to Tingley which was extended to Batley and Morley can just be made out above the locomotive.
Eric Treacy

Below:
No 60131 during its last month in BR blue livery (and not looking very clean) passes Wiske Moor water troughs at the head of the down 'Flying Scotsman'. The locomotive ran in blue for only 15 months. *E. R. Wethersett*

Bottom:
No 60131 *Osprey* near Potters Bar, heading the down 'West Riding' (King's Cross–Leeds–Bradford) express. Its carries shed code 37B (Copley Hill), which makes the picture pre-1957. *Ian Allan Library*

60131 *Osprey*

Built	Darlington October 1948 (Works No 2050)
Named	June 1950
Liveries	Originally LNER apple green with 'British Railways' on tender
	BR blue June 1950
	BR green September 1951
Allocations	King's Cross when new
	Grantham September 1951
	Copley Hill February 1953
	Ardsley April 1962
	Neville Hill July 1963
Withdrawn	4 October 1965; sold for scrap to T. W. Ward, Beighton, November 1965

Right:
After its transfer to Leeds Neville Hill shed, *Osprey* had little regular work, but, together with the other 'A1s' at the shed, worked via the Settle & Carlisle to Glasgow, usually on extra workings in the summer months. They returned to Leeds on a wide variety of trains. Here we see *Osprey* on one of these workings, the all-stations 2pm Glasgow St Enoch to Carlisle, during September 1964. The location is near Ballochmyle Viaduct on the old Glasgow & South Western main line. *T. D. Chadwicks*

Centre right:
The West Riding Branch of the Railway Correspondence & Travel Society organised a railtour from Leeds to the North East, returning via Carlisle, on 21 March 1965. *Osprey* was the locomotive allocated for the whole trip, and had been duly cleaned, but unfortunately the front numbers were not painted, which made it look odd. Heavy snow fell around Leeds, causing some passengers to miss the train, but by the time it passed Harrogate there was not a flake of snow to be seen. The locomotive gave a very poor performance during the day, dropping time with a six-coach train over the Settle & Carlisle. *Gavin Morrison*

Below:
Another view of *Osprey* on the RCTS special of 21 March 1965, this time at Stockton-on-Tees, where it made a stop for water. *Gavin Morrison*

60132 *Marmion*

Built	Darlington October 1948 (Works No 2051)
Named	December 1950
Liveries	Originally LNER apple green with 'British Railways' on tender
	BR blue November 1949
	BR green March 1952
Allocations	Gateshead when new
	Heaton May 1960
	Tweedmouth September 1962
	Gateshead December 1964
Withdrawn	14 June 1965; sold for scrap to Hughes-Bolckow, Blyth, July 1965

Above:
Marmion bursts out of Hadley Wood North Tunnel at the head of the 9.30am King's Cross–Newcastle express on 21 April 1951, looking very smart in BR blue livery. *E. D. Bruton*

Left:
Now in BR green livery, *Marmion* passes non-stop through the up centre road at Doncaster with the southbound 'Heart of Midlothian'; on the left is a Class 101 DMU ready to leave for Leeds Central. *T. Booth*

Left:
Following its last major overhaul at Doncaster Works, *Marmion* makes a fine sight as it simmers in the yard at Copley Hill shed waiting for its next duty on 12 October 1961. *Gavin Morrison*

60133 *Pommern*

Built	Darlington October 1948 (Works No 2052)
Named	April 1950
Liveries	Originally LNER apple green with 'British Railways' on tender
	BR blue April 1950
	BR green June 1952
Allocations	Grantham when new
	Copley Hill June 1950
	Ardsley September 1964
Withdrawn	21 June 1965; sold for scrap to Cox & Danks, Wadsley Bridge, August 1965

Below:
Pommern spent all but two of its 17 years allocated to the West Riding of Yorkshire, so it is not surprising that all the pictures selected show it at or south of Leeds — indeed, it was very rare to see the locomotive north of York. This early picture shows No 60133 *Pommern* on one of its regular duties, the up 'Yorkshire Pullman', near Potters Bar on 8 September 1951. Note the ex-Great Northern somersault signal on the left. *E. R. Wethersett*

Organised exhaust was being produced long before preserved lines and charter specials existed. Here the crew of *Pommern* have done an excellent job for the picture of the locomotive passing its home shed with a Leeds–King's Cross express. The picture is dated August 1952. *Eric Treacy*

Above:
A post-1957 picture, as *Pommern* now carries a 56C shedplate, at Copley Hill shed coaler, together with local 'J50' 0-6-0T No 68913. *Eric Treacy*

Below:
A powerful picture of *Pommern* accelerating away from a stop at Peterborough with a Sunday morning King's Cross–Leeds express on 2 March 1958. *P. H. Wells*

Right:
Away from its usual haunts, except when diversions were in force via Lincoln off the East Coast main line, *Pommern* is seen slipping as it leaves Lincoln Central with a Yarmouth–Leeds train on 13 July 1962. *D. C. Smith*

60134 *Foxhunter*

Built	Darlington November 1948 (Works No 2053)
Named	October 1950
Liveries	Originally LNER apple green with 'British Railways' on tender
	BR blue March 1950
	BR green February 1953
Allocations	Copley Hill when new
	Ardsley April 1962
	Neville Hill July 1965
Withdrawn	4 October 1965; sold for scrap to T. W. Ward, Beighton, November 1965

Left:
A very fine picture of No 60134 when only six months old, at the head of the down 'Yorkshire Pullman' passing New Southgate on 9 April 1949. The locomotive appears to be running without a shedplate or any indication on its buffer-beams as to where it was allocated. *E. R. Wethersett*

Right:
A pre-October 1950 picture of No 60134, on the turntable outside King's Cross station. Note the height of the coal in the tender.
Ian Allan Library

Left:
No 60134 *Foxhunter* at the head of a Leeds Central–King's Cross express, passing Little Porton on the climb to Stoke Tunnel on 7 July 1962.
Gavin Morrison

Right:
Foxhunter out of steam inside Neville Hill shed, along with active 'Q6' 0-8-0 No 63348 on 10 May 1964.
Gavin Morrison

Left:
Foxhunter waits in one of the up bay platforms at Leeds Central, with coaches to attach to the Bradford portion of a King's Cross express on 16 March 1962; this was just one month before the locomotive was transferred to Ardsley, after 13½ years at Copley Hill.
Gavin Morrison

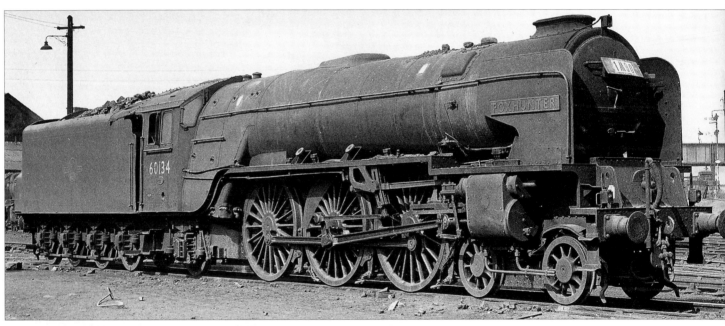

Above:
On 5 September 1963 *Foxhunter* stands at Leeds Holbeck, where members of the class could be observed simmering in the yard for days at a time, waiting for work that seldom came. It was only following its transfer to Neville Hill shed in July 1965 that *Foxhunter* was seen north of Leeds on a regular basis, when it filled its time working summer-Saturday extras to Glasgow.
Gavin Morrison

Above:
A fine pre-October 1950 portrait of No 60135, probably taken in York shed yard. As with No 60134 in the same period, there is no indication that it is allocated to Gateshead. *Eric Treacy*

Below:
No 60135, now in BR blue livery and named *Madge Wildfire*, at the head of the 2pm King's Cross–Edinburgh at Werrington troughs on 26 April 1951. *E. R. Wethersett*

60135 *Madge Wildfire*

Built	Darlington November 1948 (Works No 2054)
Named	October 1950
Liveries	Originally LNER apple green with 'British Railways' on tender
	BR blue October 1950
	BR green December 1952
Allocations	Gateshead when new
	Copley Hill November 1960
	Ardsley April 1962
Withdrawn	12 November 1962; sent to Doncaster Works for scrapping 29 May 1963

Right:
No doubt specially cleaned for the then canon's footplate ride, *Madge Wildfire* affords an impressive outlook as the locomotive powers southwards on the up 'Heart of Midlothian' between Durham and Darlington on 17 July 1952. The locomotive would probably come off at Grantham, and be replaced by a King's Cross Pacific for the final 105 miles. *Eric Treacy*

Below:
Gateshead shed must have been short of cleaners during the summer of 1959, as *Madge Wildfire* is in a terrible external condition as it heads north past Pilmoor with a down express on 16 August 1959. On the down slow line in the distance is an English Electric (later Class 08) diesel shunter. *Gavin Morrison*

Bottom:
Madge Wildfire is always remembered as a Gateshead engine, as it spent the first 12 years of its 14-year career at the depot. It subsequently had a short spell at Copley Hill, and is seen passing Wortley South Junction, Leeds, during this period at the head of an afternoon Leeds Central-King's Cross express on 1 September 1961. *Gavin Morrison*

60136 *Alcazar*

Built	Darlington November 1948 (Works No 2055)
Named	December 1950
Liveries	Originally LNER apple green with 'British Railways' on tender
	BR blue December 1950
	BR green January 1952
Allocations	Copley Hill when new
	King's Cross May 1950
	Grantham September 1951
	King's Cross April 1957
	Doncaster April 1958
	King's Cross August 1958
	Doncaster April 1959
Withdrawn	22 May 1963; sent to Doncaster Works for scrapping 29 May 1963

Below:
An early-1950s picture of No 60136 *Alcazar* passing Retford signalbox on a Leeds Central–King's Cross express, in appalling external condition. *J. Davenport*

Left:
The 'A1s', particularly the Darlington-built ones, had a reputation for rough — or possibly better described as wild — riding. *Alcazar*, it has been said, was one of the worst, and its frequent transfers within the Eastern Region might suggest that, in the 1950s, sheds were always wanting to be rid of the locomotive. It was eventually decided to carry out detailed tests between Doncaster and King's Cross in November 1957, for which *Alcazar* was fitted with an indicator shelter — the only 'A1' to be so treated. In his book *East Coast Pacifics at Work*, published by Ian Allan, P. N. Townend explains in detail the results of the tests. These concluded that the way the Darlington-built engines were assembled varied as far as tolerances were concerned from the Doncaster-built locomotives, and this, it was felt, contributed to the problem. *Alcazar* was eventually fitted with a bogie similar to those fitted to the Class A4s, and was thereafter said to ride just like an 'A4'. The rest of the class were not altered, but adjustments were made to the tolerances in setting up the cylinders. This picture, dated 1 May 1958, shows the locomotive leaving Doncaster with some empty coaches. *P. Tait*

Left:
Alcazar on top-link work at the head of the afternoon 'Talisman' from King's Cross to Edinburgh Waverley near St Neots on 9 September 1957. *E. R. Wethersett*

Top:
Easy work for *Alcazar* as it approaches Holbeck High Level station at Leeds with the 2.05pm all-stations Leeds Central to Doncaster on 30 June 1961. Farnley Junction-allocated 'Jinty' 0-6-0T No 47570 is carrying out shunting duties.
Gavin Morrison

Above:
With a clear exhaust, *Alcazar* pulls away from Wakefield

Westgate station and starts the 1 in 100 climb to Ardsley with a King's Cross-Leeds Central express on 24 August 1961. *Gavin Morrison*

Below:
With only two months to go before withdrawal, *Alcazar* looks in reasonable condition as it awaits its next duty in the yard at Doncaster shed on 24 March 1963.
Gavin Morrison

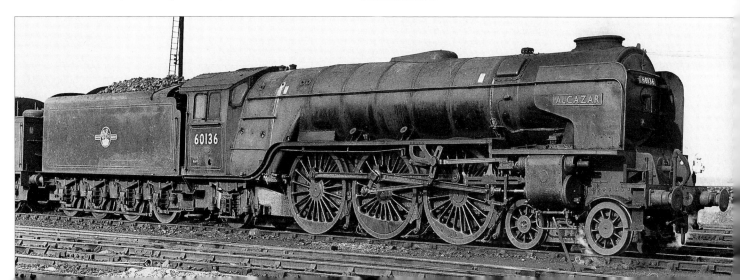

60137 *Redgauntlet*

Built	Darlington December 1948 (Works No 2056)
Named	June 1950
Liveries	Originally LNER apple green with 'British Railways' on tender
	BR blue June 1950
	BR green March 1953
Allocations	Gateshead when new
	Heaton May 1960
	Tweedmouth September 1962
Withdrawn	29 October 1962; sent to Doncaster Works for scrapping 16 April 1963

Below:
Class A8 4-6-2T No 69850 gives *Redgauntlet* a helping hand with the 5.00pm Newcastle to Liverpool Lime Street, as it was to be diverted via Wellfield. The train is seen passing Villette Road on 8 April 1956. *I. S. Carr*

Bottom:
Redgauntlet gets into its stride at the head of a down Newcastle express as it passes Hornsey in the late 1950s. A Class N2 Gresley 0-6-2T can be seen in the background. *I. S. Carr*

Right:
A travel-stained *Redgauntlet* pulls away from Newcastle on 13 April 1960 with the 4.13pm to Liverpool via Sunderland. *I. S. Carr*

Below:
Redgauntlet appears to have been an extremely camera-shy locomotive. This is surprising, as it spent 12 years at Gateshead, and should thus have been working regularly between Edinburgh and King's Cross. This picture shows it in the shed yard at York on 12 March 1962. *Gavin Morrison*

Bottom:
In poor external condition and now allocated to Heaton shed, *Redgauntlet* rounds the curve off King Edward Bridge, Newcastle, heading the 3.30pm Newcastle–Birmingham New Street on 28 May 1962. Gateshead shed, where *Redgauntlet* was allocated for 12 years, can be seen in the background. *M. Mensing*

60138 *Boswell*

Built	Darlington December 1948 (Works No 2057)
Named	September 1950
Liveries	Originally LNER apple green with 'British Railways' on tender
	BR blue September 1949
	BR green April 1952
Allocations	York when new
Withdrawn	4 October 1965; sold for scrap to T. W. Ward, Beighton, November 1965

Below:
A very fine picture of No 60138 *Boswell* ready to leave Newcastle Central with an up express. The picture is undated, but as the locomotive is in BR green livery with the original 'lion and wheel' emblem on the tender it is likely to have been taken between 1952 and 1956.
Eric Treacy

Above:
York shed must have been short of cleaners in the early 1960s, as all the pictures of *Boswell* in action show it in dirty condition. It is seen here at the head of the down 'White Rose', approaching Essendine on 8 June 1961. *P. H. Wells*

Right:
Boswell receiving an examination inside its home shed of York on 12 October 1963. The middle big-end brasses and connecting rod are dismantled. *Gavin Morrison*

Bottom right:
A rare picture of an 'A1' arriving at Birmingham New Street. The no doubt unexpected appearance of *Boswell* on the 9.20 Newcastle –Bristol has caught the attention of the enthusiasts at the station on 24 October 1964. *Ian Allan Library*

Left:
A picture of *Boswell* leaving Cambridge on the diverted 4.35pm King's Cross–York express on 8 May 1960. It had stopped at the station to set down passengers for Huntingdon, who would complete their journey by bus. *G. D. King*

Below:
No 60139 *Sea Eagle* at the head of a down express at New Southgate on 13 August 1952, during its period of allocation to Copley Hill shed. *E. R. Wethersett*

Bottom:
An extremely powerful picture of *Sea Eagle* storming up Potters Bar Bank at the head of a King's Cross–Leeds express. *Brian Morrison*

60139 *Sea Eagle*

Built	Darlington December 1948 (Works No 2058)
Named	May 1950
Liveries	Originally LNER apple green with 'British Railways' on tender
	BR blue May 1950
	BR green September 1951
Allocations	King's Cross when new
	Copley Hill July 1951
	Grantham December 1955
	King's Cross April 1957
	Doncaster April 1959
Withdrawn	7 June 1964; sold for scrap to Cox & Danks, Wadsley Bridge, January 1965

Right:
Without a hint of exhaust, *Sea Eagle* passes Milepost 200 from Edinburgh near Benningborough with an up express on the hot afternoon of 10 August 1957. *Gavin Morrison*

Right:
Sea Eagle pauses at Wakefield Westgate. The impressive tower clock shows 5.10pm, which suggests the train is the 4.50pm Leeds Central–Doncaster stopping train.
Eric Treacy

Right:
A portrait of *Sea Eagle* at its home shed of Doncaster on 15 September 1963. *Gavin Morrison*

60140 *Balmoral*

Built	Darlington December 1948 (Works No 2059)
Named	July 1950
Liveries	Originally LNER apple green with 'British Railways' on tender
	BR blue July 1950
	BR green November 1951
Allocations	York when new
	King's Cross October 1949
	York June 1950
Withdrawn	11 January 1965; sold for scrap to A. Draper, Hull, March 1965

Below:
No 60140 *Balmoral* makes a correct if somewhat unspectacular departure from Leeds Central at the head of the 12.30pm express to King's Cross on 16 March 1961. *Gavin Morrison*

Bottom:
York-allocated 'A1s' were not seen very often on Leeds Holbeck shed, but *Balmoral* was present on 15 September 1963. *Gavin Morrison*

Above:
A fine study of *Balmoral* at the head of an express to Glasgow at the north end of Newcastle Central in 1964. *M. Dunnett*

Below:
Balmoral, having just arrived at Newcastle with a Christmas relief from King's Cross on 23 December 1964. This may well have been its last main-line passenger working, as it was withdrawn only two weeks after this photograph was taken. *R. Kell*

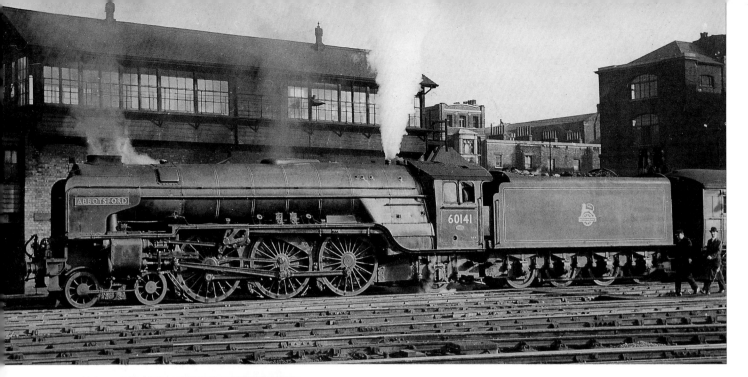

60141 *Abbotsford*

Built	Darlington December 1948 (Works No 2060)
Named	May 1950
Liveries	Originally LNER apple green with 'British Railways' on tender BR blue May 1950 BR green September 1951
Allocations	York when new King's Cross October 1949 Copley Hill May 1950 York September 1963
Withdrawn	5 October 1964; sold for scrap to A. Draper, Hull, December 1964

Above:

A fine picture of No 60141 *Abbotsford* in blue livery at the head of a down express on the afternoon of 13 October 1950, taken against the signalbox off the platform end at King's Cross. The inspector at the extreme right appears to be keeping his eye on the photographer. *C. C. B. Herbert*

Above right:

An undated portrait of *Abbotsford* at the head of an up express at Grantham. The locomotive's allocation to Copley Hill shed suggests the picture was taken after May 1950. *Ian Allan Library*

Right:

A view from the signalbox at the end of the platform shows *Abbotsford* getting to grips with the 1 in 100 climb out of Leeds Central with the up 'Yorkshire Pullman' in the early 1950s. *Eric Treacy*

Above:
An interesting location for a Class A1 sees *Abbotsford* passing Heckmondwike Junction on the ex-Lancashire & Yorkshire Cleckheaton line, during diversions of Leeds–King's Cross expresses due to engineering work around Wortley South Junction, Leeds, on 5 April 1959. *K. Field*

Right:
The shedmaster of Copley Hill in the early 1950s is quoted (in Peter Townend's *East Coast Pacifics at Work*) as claiming that *Abbotsford* was unique amongst his shed's Darlington-built 'A1s' for its good riding qualities. The locomotive is seen storming round the curve at Wortley Junction South past its home shed at the head of a King's Cross express on 7 August 1960. *Gavin Morrison*

Below:
A portrait of *Abbotsford* at York shed yard on 30 August 1964, five weeks before it was withdrawn from traffic. *Gavin Morrison*

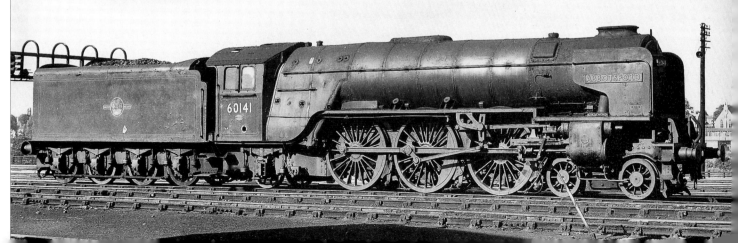

60142 *Edward Fletcher*

Built	Darlington February 1949 (Works No 2061)
Named	October 1950
Liveries	Originally LNER apple green with 'British Railways' on tender
	BR blue October 1950
	BR green December 1951
Allocation	Gateshead when new
	Heaton September 1960
	Tweedmouth September 1962
	Gateshead October 1964
Withdrawn	14 June 1965; sold for scrap to Hughes-Bolckow, Blyth, July 1965

Below:
An early picture of No 60142 *Edward Fletcher* drifting down the 1 in 190 from Burnmouth to Berwick past the Border sign with an up express. *E. R. Wethersett*

Bottom:
A powerful study of *Edward Fletcher* pulling away from Durham at the head of the up 'Northumbrian' on 7 August 1961. *I. S. Carr*

Top right:
A fine portrait of *Edward Fletcher* just out of the 'Plant' on Doncaster shed after a general overhaul on 28 August 1961. The electric lamps have been removed. The date of this photo or the previous one must be regarded with suspicion, as three weeks seems an optimistic timescale for a general overhaul. *G. Wheeler*

Right:
Surrounded by signal gantries, *Edward Fletcher* approaches Sunderland station with a down parcels train in the early 1960s. *I. S. Carr*

60143 *Sir Walter Scott*

Built	Darlington February 1949 (Works No 2062)
Named	September 1950
Liveries	Originally LNER apple green with 'British Railways' on tender BR blue September 1950 BR green October 1951
Allocations	Gateshead when new Heaton September 1960 Tweedmouth September 1962 York September 1963
Withdrawn	6 May 1964; sold for scrap to A. Draper, Hull, July 1964

Above:
A fine portrait of No 60143 *Sir Walter Scott*, showing the original style of 'lion and wheel' emblem on the tender. *Ian Allan Library*

Below:
Sir Walter Scott heads a diverted King's Cross to Edinburgh Waverley express past Bishop Auckland East on 28 October 1960. *I. S. Carr*

Above:
In immaculate condition and with sanders working, *Sir Walter Scott* leaves Tweedmouth on 9 July 1961 at the head of 1X43, the Railway Correspondence & Travel Society Border Rail Tour, which started in Leeds. The passengers enjoyed haulage behind one LMS Pacific, two LNER 'B1s', a 'J37', a preserved 'Glen', *Sir Walter Scott* and a Neville Hill 'A3' — quite a selection for a day out. *Sir Walter Scott* gave a good performance back to Newcastle, reaching 80mph near Morpeth. *Gavin Morrison*

Left:
The changing times are well illustrated in this picture taken at Newcastle. *Sir Walter Scott* has just arrived with the 9.30 Glasgow to King's Cross, while 'Deltic' No D9005 *The Prince of Wales's Own Regiment of Yorkshire* waits to take over the train on 4 March 1962. *I. S. Carr*

Below:
Only three months prior to its withdrawal, *Sir Walter Scott* stands in York shed yard on 2 February 1964. Note that the locomotive has lost its front numberplate. *Gavin Morrison*

Below:
Only one month old, No 60144 approaches Holbeck High
Level station when at the head of the 5.15pm Leeds
Central–King's Cross express on 29 April 1949. The
locomotive's allocation — Doncaster — is painted on the
buffer-beam. The curve up to Leeds Central from the low
level can just be seen on the left-hand side before the
signalbox. *H. C. Casserley*

Bottom:
Now named *King's Courier*, No 60144 climbs the 1 in 100
out of Leeds Central on the up 'White Rose' to King's Cross.
The photograph was taken during the locomotive's first
period of allocation to King's Cross 'Top Shed' in 1950/1,
although its less than pristine appearance belies this.
Eric Treacy

60144 *King's Courier*

Built	Darlington March 1949 (Works No 2063)
Named	January 1951
Liveries	Originally LNER apple green with 'British Railways' on tender
	BR blue January 1951
	BR green October 1951
Allocations	Doncaster when new
	Copley Hill December 1949
	King's Cross June 1950
	Copley Hill July 1951
	Ardsley September 1951
	Grantham February 1953
	King's Cross September 1957
	Doncaster November 1957
Withdrawn	30 April 1963; to Doncaster Works for scrapping 9 May 1963

Top right:
This picture shows the flat level
crossing of the ex-Great Central
line across the East Coast main line
at the south end of Retford station.
King's Courier heads what appears
to be a very lengthy train towards
Doncaster in May 1961, although,
on close inspection, it becomes
apparent that the rear of the train is
alongside some other coaches.
J. C. Baker

Right:
17 August 1958 found
King's Courier on its home shed of
Doncaster, where it was allocated
for its final 5½ years of service.
Gavin Morrison

Below:
Working a Penzance-Aberdeen train, No 60145 *Saint Mungo* passes Prestonpans, 10 miles south of Edinburgh Waverley, on 20 June 1952. *E. R. Wethersett*

Bottom:
Saint Mungo ready to leave York station with an up express in the late 1950s. *Ian Allan Library*

60145 *Saint Mungo*

Built	Darlington March 1949 (Works No 2064)
Named	August 1950
Liveries	Originally LNER apple green with 'British Railways' on tender
	BR blue August 1950
	BR green January 1952
Allocations	Gateshead when new
	Copley Hill November 1960
	York September 1963
	Darlington January 1966
	York April 1966
Withdrawn	19 June 1966; sold for scrap to A. Draper, Hull, August 1966

Above:
In Brunswick green livery, *Saint Mungo* makes a fine sight at the head of the up 'Queen of Scots' Pullman as it heads south past Beeston Junction, Leeds, on 7 June 1962. *Gavin Morrison*

Below:
Saint Mungo simmers gently on its home shed of Copley Hill Leeds, awaiting its next duty on 19 August 1961. The locomotive was subsequently transferred to Darlington, where, along with No 60124 *Kenilworth*, it was one of the last members of the class to be withdrawn, following use on standby duties. After withdrawal on 27 March 1966, *Saint Mungo* was reinstated on 17 April 1966 at York, being finally withdrawn on 19 June 1966. An attempt was made by Geoff Drury (one-time owner of 'A2' No 60532 *Blue Peter*) to purchase the locomotive for preservation, but unfortunately this came to naught. *Gavin Morrison*

60146 *Peregrine*

Built	Darlington April 1949 (Works No 2065)
Named	December 1950
Liveries	Originally LNER apple green with 'British Railways' on tender
	BR blue December 1950
	BR green December 1951
Allocations	Doncaster when new
	Copley Hill April 1950
	York June 1950
	Neville Hill July 1963
	York October 1963
Withdrawn	4 October 1965; sold for scrap to T. W. Ward, Killamarsh, November 1965

Below:
When only two months old, No 60146 is at the head of a Harrogate–King's Cross express at Marshmoor on 18 June 1949. In 1950 this locomotive was transferred from the Eastern Region to the North Eastern Region — an unusual occurrence except in the last few years of the class's existence. *E. R. Wethersett*

Possibly running in after a general overhaul at the 'Plant' at Doncaster, *Peregrine* passes Beeston Junction with the 10.10am semi-fast train from Leeds Central to Cleethorpes on 5 June 1962. *Gavin Morrison*

Left:
Although this superb photograph of *Peregrine* inside Leeds Central is undated, it may well have been taken minutes before the previous picture, as the locomotive is obviously ex works, and the first two coaches appear to be the same. *Eric Treacy*

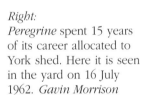

Right:
Peregrine spent 15 years of its career allocated to York shed. Here it is seen in the yard on 16 July 1962. *Gavin Morrison*

Left:
Arriving with the 10.30 Newcastle–Filey Holiday Camp, *Peregrine* presents a depressing sight at Sunderland on 8 August 1964. *I. S. Carr*

60147 *North Eastern*

Built	Darlington April 1949 (Works No 2066)
Named	March 1952
Liveries	Originally LNER apple green with 'British Railways' on tender
	BR blue November 1950
	BR green August 1951
Allocations	Gateshead when new
	Heaton September 1960
	Tweedmouth September 1962
	York September 1963
Withdrawn	28 August 1964; sold for scrap to A. Draper, Hull, December 1964

Above:
No 60147 was the penultimate member of the class to be named, and its *North Eastern* plate shows up well in this fine picture of the locomotive at the head of the up 'Flying Scotsman' at Grantham in the early 1950s. The polished buffers and general external condition suggest it may have recently been on Royal Train duties.
Ian Allan Library

Above:
North Eastern heads the down 'Heart of Midlothian' towards Pilmoor, 16 miles north of York, on 15 June 1957. *Gavin Morrison*

Right:
The driver looks relaxed as *North Eastern* climbs through Redhills cutting, just south of Durham, with the 10.10am Edinburgh Waverley–King's Cross express on 2 September 1961. *I. S. Carr*

Above:
North Eastern receiving attention inside one of the York shed roundhouses on 12 October 1963. *Gavin Morrison*

Below:
On 11 April 1964, only four months before its withdrawal, *North Eastern* has its tender filled under the coaler in York shed yard. English Electric Type 4 (Class 40) No D283 can just be seen on the right. *Gavin Morrison*

60148 *Aboyeur*

Built	Darlington May 1949 (Works No 2067)
Named	January 1951
Liveries	Originally LNER apple green with 'British Railways' on tender
	BR blue January 1951
	BR green July 1952
Allocations	Grantham when new
	King's Cross June 1950
	Grantham September 1951
	Copley Hill October 1953
	Grantham May 1954
	Copley Hill August 1955
	Ardsley September 1964
	Gateshead December 1964
	Ardsley January 1965
Withdrawn	21 June 1965; sold for scrap to Arnott Young, Dinsdale

Below:
No 60148 *Aboyeur* just about to be turned on the turntable at King's Cross ready for its next journey north. The picture was taken when the locomotive was based at Grantham in the early 1950s — note the '35B' shedplate.
Ian Allan Library

Bottom:
Another picture showing the diversions via the ex-Lancashire & Yorkshire line to Thornhill and Cleckheaton for the services between King's Cross–Bradford and Leeds, due to engineering works near Wortley Junction South. *Aboyeur* passes Horbury station, which would close to passengers on 5 January 1970, as it heads the down 'Harrogate Sunday Pullman' on 5 April 1959. *K. Field*

During its nine-year allocation to Copley Hill in the late 1950s and early 1960s, *Aboyeur* was regularly seen on the Pullman trains from Leeds. Here it is heading the up 'Queen of Scots' past Beeston station (on the outskirts of Leeds), which closed to passengers on 1 March 1953. *Gavin Morrison*

Only half a mile south of the previous picture, *Aboyeur* passes Beeston Junction heading the up 'Harrogate Sunday Pullman' on 16 April 1963. *Gavin Morrison*

60149 *Amadis*

Built	Darlington May 1949 (Works No 2068)
Named	December 1950
Liveries	Originally LNER apple green with 'British Railways' on tender
	BR blue October 1950
	BR green August 1951
Allocations	Grantham when new
	King's Cross October 1949
	Grantham March 1950
	King's Cross April 1950
	Grantham September 1951
	King's Cross September 1956
	Doncaster September 1958
Withdrawn	7 June 1964; sold for scrap to Cox & Danks, Wadsley Bridge, January 1965

Below:
A British Railways publicity photograph of *Amadis* heading the 3.15pm King's Cross–Niddrie freight through the north London suburbs on 19 June 1957. This train was regularly diagrammed for a King's Cross Pacific. *Ian Allan Library*

Bottom:
A 1950s picture of *Amadis* passing Oakleigh Park at the head of a Scarborough–King's Cross express. From the amount of coal in the tender, it would appear that the locomotive had taken over the train at Grantham. *M. W. Earley*

Above:
Doncaster was the last shed to which *Amadis* was allocated; the locomotive is shown being cleaned on shed during its six-year stay. *Ian Allan Library*

Amadis pulls away from Holbeck High Level with the 4.50pm Leeds Central–Doncaster local on 10 May 1961. This was during the period when Doncaster had more Class A1s than it could find express work for. *Gavin Morrison*

60150 *Willbrook*

Built	Darlington June 1949 (Works No 2069)
Named	January 1951
Liveries	Originally LNER apple green with 'British Railways' on tender
	BR blue January 1951
	BR green March 1952
Allocations	Heaton when new
	Gateshead July 1949
	York November 1960
Withdrawn	5 October 1964; sold for scrap to A. Draper, Hull, December 1964

Above:
No 60150 *Willbrook* rounds the curve into York station with the up 'Flying Scotsman' on 10 April 1954. It is about to cross over the lines to Scarborough, which used to cross the main line on the level. *Gavin Morrison*

Below:
Willbrook accelerates away from King Edward Bridge, Newcastle, with the up 'Flying Scotsman' in July 1954. *Eric Treacy*

Above:
After 11 years working from Gateshead, *Willbrook* was transferred to York in November 1960, but main-line work was rapidly being taken over by diesels, so there was plenty of time to clean the locomotives. Here *Willbrook* keeps company with old shedmate *Borderer*, as well as 'V2'

No 60828 and 'B1' No 61021 inside the main roundhouse at York on 11 April 1964. *Gavin Morrison*

Below:
On 30 August 1964 — two months before its withdrawal — *Willbrook* stands in the shed yard at York. *Gavin Morrison*

60151 *Midlothian*

Built	Darlington June 1949 (Works No 2070)
Named	March 1951
Liveries	Originally LNER apple green with 'British Railways' on tender
	BR blue March 1951
	BR green June 1952
Allocations	Gateshead when new
	Heaton May 1960
	Tweedmouth September 1962
	Gateshead October 1964
	York July 1965
Withdrawn	24 November 1965; sold for scrap to Station Steel, Wath, January 1966

Above:

No 60151 *Midlothian* passes Cox Green with the diverted 1.5pm Newcastle–Sunderland–King's Cross on 31 March 1957. Cox Green is between Sunderland and Ferryhill, the diversion being due to engineering work at Villette Road, Sunderland. *I. S. Carr*

Below:

A portrait of *Midlothian* taken on Gateshead shed on a murky 24 October 1964. *I. S. Carr*

Above:
A fine picture of *Midlothian* pulling out of Tyre Yard on a down freight for Edinburgh during November 1964. The main lines are in the background. *P. J. Robinson*

Below:
Midlothian has only one more journey to make — to Station Steel, of Wath. It is seen dumped in the shed yard at York, two weeks after withdrawal, on 4 December 1965. *Gavin Morrison*

60152 *Holyrood*

Built	Darlington July 1949 (Works No 2071)
Named	June 1951
Liveries	Originally LNER apple green with 'British Railways' on tender
	BR blue June 1951
	BR green November 1952
Allocations	Haymarket when new
	Polmadie January 1951
	Haymarket March 1951
	Polmadie December 1952
	Haymarket June 1953
	St Margarets September 1963
	York September 1964
Withdrawn	21 June 1965; sold for scrap to J. Cashmore, Great Bridge, August 1965

Above:
No 60152 *Holyrood* was the last of the Darlington-built 'A1s', and was also the only Darlington-built engine to be allocated new to Haymarket. It also varied from Haymarket's four other members of the class (Nos 60159-62) in that it was LNER apple green when new, whereas the others arrived in BR blue livery. The panoramic view of the west end of Edinburgh Waverley station in July 1955 shows *Holyrood* ready to leave with a train for Glasgow or the north. On the left is one of the well-kept ex-North British 'J83' 0-6-0T station pilots. *G. F. Heiron*

Right:
Apart from two short spells at Polmadie to help out on West Coast main line services, *Holyrood* spent an uninterrupted 14 years at Haymarket. In this superb picture of it passing Lady Victoria Pit at Gorebridge on the Waverley route, on a freight for Carlisle, it still has its 64B shedplate on 5 September 1963; it was transferred to St Margarets that same month. *D. Cross*

Above:
Holyrood spent its final nine months at York, although it did little work. Here it is seen in steam awaiting its next duty inside one of the roundhouses at York on 6 February 1965. *Gavin Morrison*

Below:
Another portrait of *Holyrood*, again at York shed in the yard, on 3 April 1965, 11 weeks before withdrawal. Externally it appears in good condition. *Gavin Morrison*

60153 *Flamboyant*

Built	Doncaster August 1949 (Works No 2047)
Named	August 1950
Liveries	Originally BR blue BR green December 1951
Allocations	York
Withdrawn	2 November 1962; cut up Doncaster Works 28 March 1963

Right:

Flamboyant was the first of five members of the class (Nos 60153-7) to be fitted with Timken roller-bearings on all axles. This increased the cost of each locomotive by about 23%, to £18,500. Whilst this appears to be a high figure, the costs were quickly recovered, as the mileages for these locomotives between general repairs were 18,000 miles higher than the rest of the class, at around 118,000 between heavy repairs. It was surprising, then, that this locomotive spent all its working life allocated to York, where there was less opportunity to run high mileages than at other sheds. In fact, *Flamboyant* had achieved the lowest recorded mileage of the class by the time records ceased on 5 October 1963, covering 695,122 miles to withdrawal. Other roller-bearing-fitted members had run up well over 900,000 miles.

In this picture taken at King's Cross, *Flamboyant* is ready to leave with a down express, and is well off the platform end, but near enough for the large crowd of spotters at the end of the platform to get its number. The date is September 1952. *W. J. Reynolds*

Above:
Another view of *Flamboyant* waiting to leave King's Cross with a down express, taken a few months later, in March 1953. *G. Rixon*

Left:
A fine picture of *Flamboyant* passing its home depot at York as it heads north with a down express during April 1956. Note that, compared with the other pictures of the locomotive, the position of the front numberplate has now been altered to below the handrail. *P. Ransome-Wallis*

60154 Bon Accord

Built	Doncaster September 1949 (Works No 2048)
Named	April 1951
Liveries	Originally BR blue
	BR green August 1952
Allocations	Gateshead when new
	York November 1960
	Neville Hill July 1963
Withdrawn	4 October 1965; sold for scrap to
	T. W. Ward, Killamarsh, November 1965

Below:
When only 10 months old, No 60154, the second of the roller-bearing 'A1s', makes a fine sight at the head of a down express near New Southgate in July 1950, when still in blue livery. Gateshead depot had a policy of allocating locomotives to set diagrams rather than, as at King's Cross and Haymarket, giving crews their own engines. For five years in the 1950s No 60154, alternating with No 60155, worked the up 'Night Scotsman', returning to Edinburgh the following day on the down 'Night Scotsman'. Occasionally King's Cross would borrow these locomotives for a return trip to Grantham or Peterborough as well, so they could be covering 510 miles in 24 hours. These workings over this five-year period must have been the finest performances for the class, both of course being roller-bearing locomotives, although initially No 60157 *Great Eastern* held the mileage record, covering 693,563 miles between entering service in November 1949 and its fifth heavy intermediate repair in October 1958. *E. R. Wethersett*

Bottom:
An undated portrait of *Bon Accord*, apparently in ex-works condition and believed to be at the south end of Grantham station. *Ian Allan Library*

Left:
An unusual sighting of *Bon Accord* on a night sleeper/postal train, the 10.35 King's Cross to Edinburgh Waverley, travelling via the North British Waverley route at Borthwick due to flooding on the East Coast main line, on 29 August 1956. Judging by the coal in the tender, it must have taken over the train at Newcastle. *Ian S. Pearsall*

Left:
Another picture of *Bon Accord* away from its regular duties on the main line. Here it is seen near Pontefract, drifting down the bank towards Pontefract Baghill station heading the 8.30am Cardiff–Newcastle on 7 September 1957. *P. Cookam*

Below:
Bon Accord had been allocated to Leeds Neville Hill for only two months when this picture was taken at Leeds Holbeck depot on 14 September 1963. By this time, the Class A1s at Neville Hill had little work; this locomotive and others of the allocation could often be seen during the week at Holbeck, waiting for diesel failures on a Settle & Carlisle working, which by the end of 1963 was relatively infrequent. At weekends they occasionally reached Glasgow St Enoch via the Glasgow & South Western, and took some time making their way back to Leeds. *Gavin Morrison*

60155 *Borderer*

Built	Doncaster September 1949 (Works No 2049)
Named	March 1951
Liveries	Originally BR blue
	BR green May 1952
Allocations	Gateshead when new
	Heaton September 1960
	Tweedmouth September 1962
	York November 1962
Withdrawn	4 October 1965; sold for scrap to
	T. W. Ward, Killamarsh, November 1965

Below:
The fact that neither the extensive Ian Allan photographic library nor the author's own collection contain a picture of No 60155 *Borderer* taken before 1 August 1961 is probably a reflection of the time this roller-bearing-fitted 'A1' spent working the 'Night Scotsman' during the 1950s. The locomotive is seen near Beeston on the 2.05pm all-stations Leeds Central to Doncaster, probably after visiting Doncaster for works attention. *Gavin Morrison*

Bottom:
Whilst allocated to Heaton shed in Newcastle, *Borderer* finds itself on mundane duties as it heads an up freight near Benningborough on 24 April 1962. Such work was hardly suitable for a roller-bearing 'A1', but by this date all but one of the 'Deltics' were in action, so its old main line duties at Gateshead had been taken over. *J. K. Morton*

Above:
7 April 1963 saw *Borderer* awaiting its next duty at the south end of Doncaster shed. *Gavin Morrison*

Right:
A superb study of *Borderer* in excellent external condition on 25 July 1964 — possibly because by that date it was doing very little work at its home depot of York — preparing to leave Newcastle with the 10.25am Scarborough–Glasgow Queen Street express, which it probably worked between York and Edinburgh. *M. Dunnott*

Below:
On 30 August 1964 *Borderer* was in light steam in the yard of York shed awaiting its next duty, which by that date may have been some time in coming.
Gavin Morrison

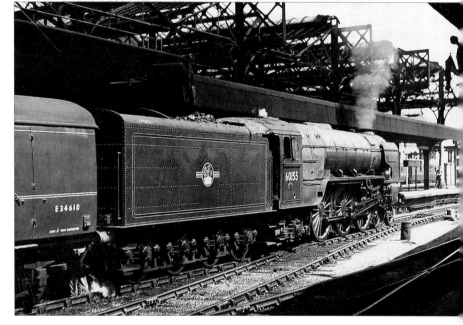

60156 *Great Central*

Built	Doncaster October 1949 (Works No 2050)
Named	July 1952
Liveries	Originally BR blue
	BR green July 1952
Allocations	King's Cross when new
	Grantham September 1951
	King's Cross September 1956
	Doncaster April 1959
	York January 1964
Withdrawn	10 May 1965; sold for scrap to Cox & Danks, Wadsley Bridge, June 1965

Below:
No 60156 *Great Central* passes non-stop through York on the down 'Flying Scotsman' and captures the attention of a group of school children enjoying a day's observation at the north end of the station on 10 April 1956. P. N. Townend, in his excellent book *East Coast Pacifics at Work*, comments in one of the captions about *Great Central* that, when it was allocated to two regular drivers at King's Cross, it was considered by them to be the finest Pacific at the shed — an opinion (this author suspects) not shared by the regular drivers of the Class A4s — and, being one of the members of the class fitted with roller-bearings, ran very high mileages. *Gavin Morrison*

Left:
Regrettably no details are available for the following selection of pictures of *Great Central*, but all must have been taken in the mid-1950s as the locomotive bears the original 'lion and wheel' emblem on the tender. In this view it is climbing Holloway Bank at the head of a down express. *Eric Treacy*

Above:
Great Central appears to be ex works as it leaves Doncaster on an up stopping train. The photograph was probably taken in July 1952 when the locomotive first received green livery and was allocated to Grantham shed. *Eric Treacy*

Below:
Great Central being turned outside King's Cross station prior to leaving with the down 'Aberdonian'. *Eric Treacy*

Below:
A superb picture of No 60157, the last of the roller-bearing locomotives, in blue livery. It is leaving Newcastle on what is most likely a King's Cross express. The King's Cross shedplate suggests that the photograph was taken before September 1951. *Eric Treacy*

Bottom:
Now allocated to Grantham, repainted in BR green livery and named *Great Eastern*, No 60157 is seen at its home shed on 4 October 1953. *B. K. B. Green*

60157 *Great Eastern*

Built	Doncaster November 1949 (Works No 2051)
Named	November 1951
Liveries	Originally BR blue
	BR green November 1951
Allocations	King's Cross when new
	Grantham September 1951
	King's Cross September 1956
	Doncaster April 1959
Withdrawn	10 January 1965; sold for scrap to A. Draper, Hull, February 1965

Above:
There are no details with this fine photograph, but it shows an immaculate *Great Eastern* leaving what is probably Welwyn Tunnel on the down 'Tees-Tyne Pullman'. The locomotive carries a King's Cross shedplate.
Ian Allan Library

Top right:
Now carrying the later 'lion and wheel' emblem, *Great Eastern* appears to be going well at the head of the down 'West Riding' express, loaded to at least 12 coaches, seen between Potters Bar and Brookmans Park. *D. Cross*

Middle right:
At the head of an Ian Allan special, *Great Eastern* emerges from Marsh Lane Cutting at Leeds, having worked the train from King's Cross on 26 April 1958. The train continued over the Pennines via the Standedge route headed by two of the last Midland Compounds. *Gavin Morrison*

Bottom right:
Great Eastern about to back off Holbeck shed at Leeds to work a local train back to Doncaster. The picture was taken in October 1964 when the locomotive had only three months left in service. *Gavin Morrison*

Left:
An extremely powerful picture of Great Central. Some readers will no doubt be able to identify the location, but there are no details available. *R. K. Evans*

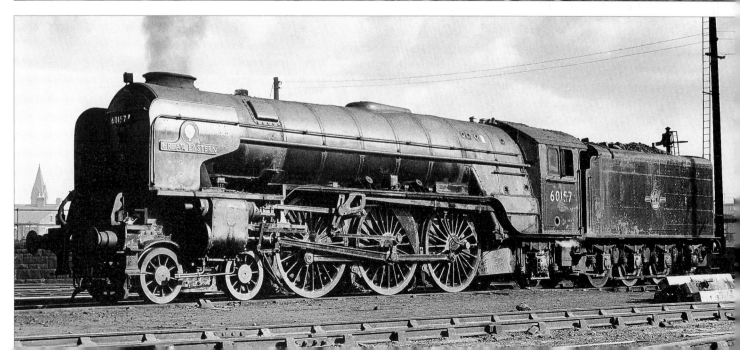

Below:
A month before its transfer away from King's Cross,
No 60158 *Aberdonian* stands at the head of an up express
at Aycliffe on 2 August 1951, whilst still in blue livery.
E. R. Wethersett

Bottom:
The crew have obviously been asked to make sure there is
a good exhaust from *Aberdonian* as it passes Wortley South,
Leeds, on the 5.15pm Leeds Central–King's Cross in July
1952. *Eric Treacy*

60158 *Aberdonian*

Built	Doncaster November 1949 (Works No 2052)
Named	March 1951
Liveries	Originally BR blue
	BR green November 1952
Allocations	King's Cross when new
	Grantham September 1951
	Copley Hill June 1953
	Grantham May 1954
	King's Cross June 1957
	Doncaster September 1958
Withdrawn	26 December 1964; sold for scrap to
	Hughes-Bolckow, Blyth, February 1965

Above:
With at least 13 coaches behind the tender, *Aberdonian* makes a very clean departure from York past Holgate Bridge with the up 'Northumbrian'. *Eric Treacy*

Below:
Aberdonian prepares to leave Doncaster on an up van train in the mid-1950s. *B. Green*

60159 *Bonnie Dundee*

Built	Doncaster November 1949 (Works No 2053)
Named	July 1951
Liveries	Originally BR blue
	BR green December 1952
Allocations	Haymarket when new
	St Margarets September 1963
Withdrawn	14 October 1963; cut up Inverurie Works
	January 1964

Below:
No 60159 *Bonnie Dundee* pulls out of Edinburgh Waverley at the head of an express for Aberdeen on 28 July 1955. Like No 60162 *Saint Johnstoun, Bonnie Dundee* spent all its working career allocated to Haymarket, and in the 1950s was the engine allocated to Driver Proudfoot, another well-known Haymarket character. Having their own dedicated crews was probably the reason *Bonnie Dundee* and *Saint Johnstoun* didn't have spells at Polmadie depot in Glasgow. *G. F. Heiron*

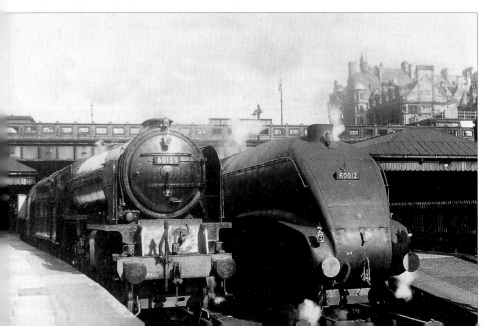

Left:
Two of Haymarket's well-known Pacifics side-by-side at the west end of Edinburgh Waverley station, waiting to leave with trains for the north. Class A4 No 60012 *Commonwealth of Australia* had already put in 12 years' service at Haymarket by the time *Bonnie Dundee* arrived at the end of 1949. Both locomotives were in No 2 link with regular crews in the 1950s, although the external condition of No 60012 is not up to the usual standard. *Bonnie Dundee*, on the other hand, positively sparkled, no doubt due to the efforts of Driver Proudfoot and his fireman. This undated picture must have been taken before July 1958 as No 60012 had not yet been fitted with a double chimney.
Ian Allan Library

Above:
Bonnie Dundee and 'A4' No 60011 *Empress of India* had
been stablemates at Haymarket depot for 11 years when this
picture was taken in the shed on 31 December 1960. Their
regular main-line duties were soon to be taken over by
'Deltics', and English Electric Type 4s (later Class 40) were
already around. Nevertheless they made a fine sight at the
east end of the shed, awaiting their next workings. In the
background are a couple of BRCW Type 2s (Class 26),
which had already put in a couple of years' service.
C. W. Robertson

Below:
The north end of Newcastle Central sees *Bonnie Dundee*
taking water before heading off north. The date is 2 August
1961, a few months after 'Deltics' had taken over most of
Haymarket's East Coast main line diagrams, so the Pacifics
were obviously not receiving the attention they once
enjoyed. *Gavin Morrison*

60160 *Auld Reekie*

Built	December 1949 (Works No 2054)
Named	March 1951
Liveries	Originally BR blue
	BR green March 1953
Allocations	Haymarket when new
	Polmadie January 1951
	Haymarket March 1951
	Polmadie September 1951
	Haymarket February 1952
	St Margarets September 1963
Withdrawn	12 December 1963; cut up
	Darlington Works 9 March 1964

Below:
An early undated photograph of No 60160 *Auld Reekie*, with the fireman appearing to be breaking up large lumps of coal on the tender. It will be noted from the allocations that along with Nos 60152 and 60161, *Auld Reekie* had short spells at Polmadie in the early 1950s for working the West Coast main line from Glasgow to Crewe. *Ian Allan Library*

Below:
A fine study of *Auld Reekie* at Doncaster Works on 22 March 1953 outside the paint shops after a general repair. *P. H. Wells*

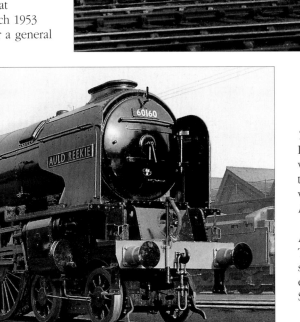

Top right:
During July 1955 *Auld Reekie* threads its way over the complicated trackwork at the west end of Edinburgh Waverley with an express from the north. *Ian Allan Library*

Bottom right:
The west end of Edinburgh Waverley sees *Auld Reekie* ready to leave with an express, probably for Glasgow Queen Street, in the 1950s. *Ian Allan Library*

Right:
Auld Reekie catches the evening sun as it descends the 1 in 41 gradient down Cowlairs Bank at the head of the 3pm Edinburgh Waverley to Glasgow Queen Street express in March 1955. *Gavin Morrison*

Above:
A fine study of *Auld Reekie* at the head of the 'Heart of Midlothian', probably taken in the woods between Cockburnspath and Grantshouse. Just a wisp of steam from the safety valve and a trace of exhaust suggests all was well on the footplate. *Ian Allan Library*

Below:
Although still allocated to Haymarket, *Auld Reekie's* days of careful maintenance and cleaning are over, as it works out its last six months of service. It is seen leaving Motherwell on 20 June 1963, at the head of the 9.50 Euston–Perth, having probably been substituted for a failed 'Princess Coronation' by Carlisle Kingmoor shed. *M. Bryce*

60161 *North British*

Built	Doncaster December 1949 (Works No 2055)
Named	June 1951
Liveries	Originally BR blue
	BR green November 1952
Allocations	Haymarket when new
	Polmadie January 1951
	Haymarket March 1951
	Polmadie September 1951
	Haymarket June 1953
	St Margarets September 1963
Withdrawn	28 October 1963; cut up Inverurie Works
	February 1964

Below:
This undated picture, probably taken in the early 1950s, shows No 60161 *North British* still with its original chimney, waiting to back off Haymarket shed to work a train north from Edinburgh Waverley. Class B1 No 61404, another local engine, is in the background. No 60161, along with Nos 60152 and 60160, had short spells allocated to Polmadie, when they worked the evening 6.25pm post to Crewe, returning the following day on the 12.50 Birmingham–Glasgow. Photographs of the locomotives working the West Coast main line are not easy to find. Presumably the reason for the transfers was that Polmadie was short of Stanier Pacifics. *Ian Allan Library*

Another view of *North British* in Haymarket shed, showing the impressive badge on the locomotive's nameplate. *Ian Allan Library*

Above:
A fine study of *North British* waiting at the east end of Edinburgh Waverley station, ready to work the 'Queen of Scots' Pullman to Newcastle, which it would take over from one of Eastfield's Class B1s or Standard '5MTs'. *Eric Treacy*

Below:
North British leaves Edinburgh Waverley at the head of a train for Perth on 7 October 1954. *T. Lovegrove*

60162 *Saint Johnstoun*

Built	Doncaster 1949 (Works No 2056)
Named	August 1951
Liveries	Originally BR blue
	BR green August 1951
Allocations	Haymarket when new
	St Margarets September 1963
Withdrawn	14 October 1963; cut up Inverurie
	Works March 1964

Below:
Looking in its customary immaculate external condition, No 60162 *Saint Johnstoun* stands at its home depot of Haymarket (64B), Edinburgh, in September 1953. As the photograph shows, the locomotive's original chimney was still in place at this time. *J. Robertson*

Right:
Saint Johnstoun was regularly seen at the head of the up 'Queen of Scots' Pullman between Edinburgh Waverley and Newcastle Central, and is pictured about to leave the Scottish capital on this working in 1954. The photographer comments on the back of the print that it was the cleanest locomotive in the British Isles. This is possibly a slightly extravagant claim, but the locomotive was certainly kept in immaculate condition by its regular driver at this time, Willie Bain, and his fireman. It is fair to say that this was also the case with many of the other Haymarket Pacifics in the 1950s which were allocated regular crews. The same was true in Glasgow, where many of the Fairburn and Standard 2-6-4Ts from Polmadie also had their regular crews.
Ian Allan Library / Loco Publishing

Left:
A fine picture of *Saint Johnstoun* leaving Newcastle Central on the King's Cross–Glasgow Queen Street, known as the 'Junior Scotsman'. The locomotive is in its usual sparkling external condition. Note the complex track layout and all the signals under the station roof. The picture is undated, but was probably taken in the mid-1950s. *Eric Treacy*

Left:
Saint Johnstoun approaches Reston on an up Saturday extra on 15 July 1961. This picture has been included to show the locomotive in terrible external condition — a state in which it was seldom photographed. By this time, 'Deltics' and EE Type 4s had taken over many of the express diagrams, and the old standards of cleanliness at Haymarket had vanished. *Gavin Morrison*

Below:
The five regular Haymarket 'A1s' — Nos 60152/9-62 — were seldom seen south of Newcastle, except for works visits to Doncaster. On 20 July 1962 *Saint Johnstoun* made what was probably the only visit of a Scottish 'A1' to Leeds Holbeck, having apparently stood in for a failed 'Peak' diesel-electric on one of the up Scottish sleepers during the night. Its external appearance is a great improvement over that of a year earlier. *Gavin Morrison*

The A1 Steam Locomotive Trust

Registered Office, General Correspondence & Membership Enquiries: Darlington Railway Centre & Museum, North Road Station, Darlington DL3 6ST
Hotline Answerphone: 01325 460163

THE BUILDING OF TORNADO —
AN UPDATE ON THE A1 PROJECT'S PROGRESS
by Mark Allatt, Chairman, and David Elliott, Chief Engineer

The A1 Steam Locomotive Trust was set up in 1990 to right an infamous wrong: the wholesale scrapping of the final development of the East Coast main line's express passenger steam locomotives — the Peppercorn Class A1 Pacifics.

With construction of No 60163 *Tornado* having commenced in 1994 with the profiling of the mainframes by BSD, the steel stockholding arm of British Steel (now Corus), the time is probably right to take stock and examine what has been achieved and what has yet to be done.

David Champion, former chairman of the A1 Steam Locomotive Trust, used to say that the only way to eat an elephant is in small pieces — and that is the way that the Trust has tackled the construction of the 50th Peppercorn Class A1.

History of the 'A1s'
The original 49 Peppercorn Class A1s were designed by the LNER and built for British Railways in 1948/9. As designed, they were ideally suited for the postwar world of poor maintenance and heavy trains, with their 50sq ft grate allowing them to use lower-grade coal than did their predecessors. The final five were even equipped with roller-bearings, enabling them to go for an average of 118,000 miles between heavy repairs, making the 'A1s' the cheapest to run of all British steam locomotives in the same category.

Unfortunately, the rapid onset of dieselisation in the 1960s meant that all 49 were scrapped, after an average life of only 15 years. There was an attempt to save the last survivor, No 60145 *Saint Mungo*, but this unfortunately failed and it too was withdrawn in June 1966 and scrapped that September. As there was no Barry Scrapyard for ex-LNER locomotives, here the story would probably have ended.

The Launch of the A1 Project
Following a letter to a railway magazine, the project to build the 50th Class A1 was launched to a packed meeting in York in November 1990, and this was followed by further presentations in London and Edinburgh.
The organisation of what was to become the largest single project in railway preservation in Britain today was based around four principles:

1. It would have to be run using the best business practices by people experienced in the appropriate areas.
2. The funding method would have to be simple, and capable of being understood and afforded by virtually anyone.
3. Because of the enormity of the task, there would have to be a single aim on which to focus — the Project's Mission Statement, 'To build and operate a Peppercorn Class A1 Pacific steam locomotive for main-line and preserved railway use' — against which all proposed actions would be judged.
4. The rules of the organisation would prohibit cliques and any form of élitism. Everyone would achieve recognition based on effort rather than size of chequebook. This would enable all efforts to go into the building of the 'A1'.

A nationwide management team was put together — engineers, accountants, solicitors, bankers, marketeers and other appropriate professionals — which has been continually bolstered as the project has progressed.

Design and Construction
The Trust's approach to constructing a new steam locomotive in the 1990s builds on what has already been achieved by the railway preservation movement. Since the end of steam on British Railways in 1968, the movement has manufactured almost all of the components necessary to build a new main-line steam locomotive in separate restoration projects, including:

- rebuilding total hulks from Barry Scrapyard
- casting new cylinders
- casting new driving wheels
- building new boilers and fireboxes
- constructing a number of new narrow gauge and replica early steam locomotives.

The only difference with the A1 Project is the scale and the fact that all of the components are brand new.

The Project's technical team has carried out an enormous amount of research, not only into the 'A1s' but also into the manufacturing techniques and the steam design philosophy of the 1940s. Using the latest Computer Aided Design (CAD) technology, with the help of Rasterex UK, over 1,100 separate original drawings from the National Railway Museum's archives have been scanned onto computer, allowing them to be cleaned up, modified and printed when needed.

Due to the time which has elapsed since the building of the 49th 'A1', it has not been possible for the 50th to be simply a replica. Change in material specifications, cost and regulations prevent this. However, the Trust has resolved that the twin criteria of authenticity and quality must apply to all decisions on specification and construction. The only area of major redesign identified is that of the boiler, where for reasons of cost, regulation and lack of capacity to rivet a structure the size of an 'A1' boiler, the decision has been made to redesign the boiler as an all-welded structure with a steel firebox.

In addition to the need for authenticity, to allow the locomotive to work on main-line and preserved railways in the UK or abroad it has to satisfy modern Railtrack requirements, meet modern safety regulations, and gain insurance company approval. Therefore the manufacture of the locomotive is being organised in accordance with ISO9000 standards.

Finance and Sponsorship
When the Project was launched in 1990 it was estimated that the locomotive would cost around £1 million to build over a 10-year period. The effects of inflation have now increased this figure to £1.7 million. The method of funding this amount was designed to be as simple as possible. The

Trust is using two complementary methods, namely Covenants to the Trust, and Industrial Sponsorship and Benefits in Kind.

The concept of covenanting to the Trust is based on the idea of a lot of people giving a little on a regular basis — a concept that can be understood by anyone and afforded by virtually everyone. The slogan "An 'A1' for the Price of a Pint" is based on members' covenanting the price of a pint of beer a week (£1.25 in the North East when the project was launched!). Thus for units of £5 per month (some people covenant considerably more) a brand-new 'A1' will be built. As a registered charity, the Trust can reclaim income tax from the Inland Revenue for every covenanted subscription it receives, grossing up each contribution by a factor of 28% (based on a basic rate of income tax of 22%). Thus, for every £1 covenanted, £1.28 is received by the Trust, giving a very efficient and effective way of funding the work and turning each £5 into £6.40. Although it would be possible to build the locomotive using just covenants, significant benefits in kind and sponsorship are expected to make the desired completion date of December 2003 a reality.

The Trust actively seeks industrial sponsorship, the donations of benefits in kind and work at concessionary rates. It has been very fortunate over the past few years to secure the support of many organisations, whose help, in various ways, will enable it to complete the locomotive:

- Macreadys, the leading steel-bar stockholder, is providing the Trust with a variety of steels from its wide stock range, including bright round bars for use as pins, bushes and shafts on the new locomotive.
- William Cook PLC, the world's leading steel foundry group, is making the pattern equipment, casting and machining No 60163's six 6ft 8in-diameter driving wheels on 'very advantageous terms' to the Trust.
- British Steel PLC met the vast majority of the cost of the specially-rolled steel plate (supplied by British Steel) for the main frames. BSD Plate & Profile Products, Leeds, profiled the main frames. British Steel Engineering completed the casting of three complex cylinder castings at very advantageous rates.
- Timken Rail Bearing Systems has supplied modern equivalents of the original Timken roller bearings at a beneficial price and has provided technical support free of charge.
- Charles Taylor & Co of South Shields has cast a number of smokebox components, including the chimney and blastpipe, free of charge.

In addition, a number of other companies have kindly supplied the Trust with packings, gaskets and seals; drawing office and machine shop time; use of a Computer Aided Design System and laser scanner; welding equipment with gas and air; blue, green and black paint for *Tornado*'s top coats; and the creation, updating and running of the Trust's Internet site. Further offers are keenly sought, and will appreciably speed the locomotive's construction.

Progress to Date
- Over half of the required covenants now in place and increasing rapidly
- Over 1,100 original drawings identified in the National Railway Museum and scanned on to the Project's Computer-Aided Design system
- BR Mk1 BSK No 35457 purchased for use as a support coach and overhauled and refurbished

- Main frame plates rolled May 1994 and profiled July 1994
- Frame stretcher patterns constructed and all 21 frame stretchers cast/fabricated and fitted
- Inside-cylinder pattern delivered December 1994 and inside cylinder cast August 1995
- Driving- and carrying-wheel patterns manufactured and all six driving wheels cast by August 1995
- Outside cylinders cast April 1996
- mainframes substantially complete with inside cylinder in place and much of the footplating attached; fabrication of cab nearing completion
- Permanent home in Darlington, converted into 'Darlington Locomotive Works'
- Frames moved from Tyseley to Darlington September 1997
- Smokebox components made in 1998/9
- Smokebox fitted to locomotive November 1999
- Wheelsets assembled 1998/9 by Riley & Son at Bury
- Reversing gear forged 1999, machined 2000
- Pistons, crossheads, coupling and connecting rods manufactured and machined early 2000
- Locomotive wheeled and rods fitted Summer 2000

Challenges for 2000/1
The construction of *Tornado* can effectively be divided into three basic units — the frames, the wheelsets and motion, and the boiler. The first of these was completed at Tyseley Locomotive Works in Birmingham. Bob Meanley and his team burned the midnight oil to get *Tornado* ready for its move to Darlington in September 1997.

The wheelsets are complete following a long and complex series of processes masterminded by Ian Riley at the East Lancs Locomotive Works at Bury. This involved resurrecting the traditional process of pressing wheels onto axles. The motion is well underway, with all the large forgings being machined at present. The total cost of the motion is in the order of £110,000.

The boiler remains a major obstacle to be surmounted. Although not technically challenging — many new boilers have been built for preserved locomotives and a design for an all-welded boiler is in hand — the expected cost of around £250,000 is certainly a challenge! The Trust is currently putting together sponsor-partners and covenanted income to fund this part of the project, but much remains to be done before we can be confident that the challenge has been met.

It could be said that the Trust is within sight of having a partially-completed ex-Barry locomotive to restore, with overhauled frames, wheels and the shell of a boiler. Once we have cracked the boiler we will have just that, and all know how much work will still remain to be done — although at least everything we have will be in brand-new condition.

The Trust has eaten over half of David Champion's elephant since its foundation in 1990. We now need help in finishing it off, and there are a couple of big joints to go yet. More covenantors, sponsors and volunteers are needed to get *Tornado* in steam. We look forward to hearing from you.

Further information on the A1 Steam Locomotive Trust and an application form to become a covenantor can be obtained from the Covenant Officer, The A1 Steam Locomotive Trust, Darlington Railway Centre & Museum, North Road Station, Darlington DL3 6ST, or by telephoning our 24-hour Hotline on 01325 460163.

Right:
Frames for *Tornado* just after cutting in Leeds, 7 September 1994.
Gavin Morrison

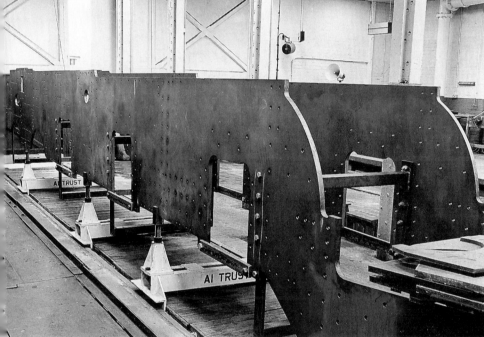

Left:
Frames at Tyseley Locomotive Works, 5 January 1995.
Gavin Morrison

Right:
Pattern for cylinder at Tyseley, 5 January 1995. *Gavin Morrison*